T0330286

# Small Law; Big Success

# Small Law;
# Big Success

How to Use Business Niche Specialization
to Grow a Multi-Million Dollar Law
Practice

Yussuf Aleem

Jacob Slowik

*Joseph, Aleem & Slowik, LLC, USA*

 Edward Elgar
PUBLISHING

Cheltenham, UK ● Northampton, MA, USA

Published by
Edward Elgar Publishing Limited
The Lypiatts
15 Lansdown Road
Cheltenham
Glos GL50 2JA
UK

Edward Elgar Publishing, Inc.
William Pratt House
9 Dewey Court
Northampton
Massachusetts 01060
USA

A catalogue record for this book
is available from the British Library

Library of Congress Control Number: 2018958449

This book is available electronically in the **Elgar**online
Law subject collection

DOI 10.4337/9781788973908

ISBN 978 1 78897 389 2 (cased)
ISBN 978 1 78897 391 5 (paperback)
ISBN 978 1 78897 390 8 (eBook)

Typeset by Columns Design XML Ltd, Reading
Printed on FSC approved paper
Printed and bound in Great Britain by Marston Book Services Ltd, Oxfordshire

# Contents

# Acknowledgments

Yussuf

To my mother and late father, who forged my character and deserve unending credit for my accomplishments. This undertaking would also not be possible without the immense support of my mentors, Tarek Aleem, Esq. and Mohamad Ahmad, Esq., and encouragement from Audrey Jouve, Esq., Munish Dayal, Esq., Ray Kermani, Esq., Omar Aleem, and Mehdi Eddebbarh, Esq.

Jacob

To my mother, brother and Charlie, for their unwavering love and support.

To Joe T., who first acknowledged a desire to have me join the profession, offered me my first opportunity in the legal industry, and who first taught me the business of the law.

To Jon M., who taught me what it was to find fulfilment in a legal career and live a passion for the law.

To Tarek A., who provides an eternal spark to action.

To Richard H., for his gritty and witty insights and feedback.

# 1. Introduction

We were both advised that the practice of law was one of the safest career paths to achieve success, prestige, and wealth. We were told that, for those who chose to pursue this path, the journey to those rewards would be straightforward: attend law school, focus on litigation or corporate transactions, fight tooth and nail for a job at a respected firm, and bust your butt to make partner. Further, we were advised, the only sure path to the higher echelons of law is through the doors of *BigLaw*, a term we use throughout this book, which refers, collectively, to the nation's largest and most success-ful law firms. It was understood by most around us that only these BigLaw firms represent the best, the most successful, and the elite. And in order to even have a chance of reaching that rarified status, we must devote the best years of our lives to working for BigLaw.

We had a hunch that this conventional wisdom about a legal career was flawed, at best, and deliberately manipulative, at worst. We came to believe that there was in fact a better route to career prosperity. We seemed to continuously read or hear stories of how this startup disrupted that industry. How this seemingly "regular" girl hacked a routine and was able to get 100 times the result in a fraction of the time. How another man turned expectations upside down and now works only a few hours a week making three times as much money as he used to. We read these success stories and bemoaned that the law seemed to be the last industry to the "disrupt party."

Adopting this "disrupt" mindset, we went out and "hacked" the legal industry to create the career we wanted. With technology now putting unprecedented amounts of information at anyone's finger-tips, the institutional dynamics of the legal industry had already been changed forever and were primed for a shift. We found out, through strategic thinking, myth-busting, creativity, and hard work, that we could build a very successful career in law without sacrificing too many years of our lives in BigLaw. We discovered an innovative strategy and accompanying tactics that are suited to the smaller size, greater agility, and other advantages of an independent firm and that can forge a path that is unconventional, but at least as effective, to that pinnacle of success. And we're going to tell you how we did it so that you can learn from our experience and do it yourself.

We learned to leave the conventional wisdom and beliefs about how to achieve career prosperity behind us. That old conventional wisdom appeared to be supported by an entrenched hierarchy that primarily serves to maximize the needs of the BigLaw firms rather than our own career fulfilment. We resolved that if we wanted success in a law career on our own terms, we needed to transcend the conventional route and go beyond BigLaw.

If you've been working in BigLaw and you're tired, disillusioned, frustrated, or just fed up, you're not alone. If you're turned off by the scarcity of respect, the culture of anonymity, and a shocking lack of opportunities to build your career for the long term, and believe that it's not likely to change for many years to come, we and many others have been right there with you. If you find yourself on the precipice of graduating law school without a solid job prospect or if you are in a middling firm or a middling place within a large firm, without any agency over the future of your career, we empathize with you and want to offer you our experience. We want to tell you our story of how we flipped the script on the conventional legal career "wisdom."

Being smart and industrious by nature, you probably spent quite a number of years energized to follow the advice of your parents, teachers, professors, and mentors who told you to toe the line, work hard, be a team player, and have faith that your hard work will pay off in the long run. You hunkered down, lived on cheaper and junkier food, spent less time with your family, abandoned your social life, and likely risked your health, all in the service of advancing your legal career. With great resolve, you wanted to do what it took to make it.

If you are like us, the overt and covert messages you got from those around you were undeniable: the best way to achieve all that you desire is to devote yourself to life in a large law firm. Only on the shoulders of a highly respected, established practice can you get the experience, the connections, and the successes that it promises you. Then, and only then, can you finally arrive.

And of course you set your sites on the pinnacle of success as an American attorney: partnership in a BigLaw firm. Get your name on the partners list. Relish the peerless prestige of the position. Enjoy all the benefits that a stratospheric starting salary can give you: first class office space, an impressive reputation, the cars and homes of your dreams, extraordinary vacations, and the respect you deserve.

But there's a wrinkle in this vision. Each year, thousands of law school graduates and young lawyers awaken to the fact that the rich and rewarding career in law that they envisioned for themselves just won't materialize as easily or as quickly as they expected it would, if at all. The job market is fiercely competitive. Well-paying legal positions – especially those in BigLaw – are not anywhere near as accessible as they had hoped.

Many of the lawyers working for BigLaw are disillusioned with what they experience there. New hires are typically required to suffer through extraordinary sacrifices, grueling hours, and acceptance of a culture of jealous competition. Worse yet, the odds of your hard work paying off with an offer of a non-equity partnership position are not amazing.[1] Those of equity partner even worse.[2] The numbers don't add up in your favor.

If you find yourself convinced that BigLaw is the best path for you to achieve a fulfilling legal career, we are happy you have found that resolve and we sincerely hope for the best for you. We are not writing this book to attempt to convince you otherwise. We certainly have several friends and colleagues who have come to that same conclusion and we are happy to hear about and actively root for their progress in BigLaw. We came to our own conclusions about BigLaw and the conventional legal career prospects available to us and we encourage all to undertake their own examination and come to their own conclusions as well. This book will tell the story of how we understood the legal career options available to us and our story of how we forged a different path (and, we believe, a better path). We are not attempting to make the case against BigLaw or any other career options for you – there are plenty of resources that will provide the data and analysis for you to

---

[1] http://amlawdaily.typepad.com/amlawdaily/2012/03/the-big-law-partner-lottery.html

[2] Id.

determine that on your own. If, however, you are interested in hearing about a different path to legal career success, we write to share our story, to identify the strategy that we pursued and to discuss the tactics we used to implement that strategy and ultimately found legal career success and fulfilment on our terms.

* * *

We say we have found another way – a *better* way – for us to achieve the prosperity and accomplishments that we sought as attorneys. We know this because we have done it. We have a stable roster of clients; we have the respect as one of the leading law firms within our business niche; we've paid off all of our student loans; and have savings that bring financial security.

Now we want to show you how you we arrived here so that you may glean from our blueprint a strategy and tactics that may empower you to achieve the success you seek as a lawyer too, and on your own terms.

We'll teach you how we "hacked" the legal profession to take control of our individual legal careers and find success on our terms. We'll teach you how we retooled our legal career paths to maximize financial security, independence, and expertise. We'll teach you how we disrupted the traditional legal career path in the legal career industry to forge our own success, so you can too.

We'll teach you how the size, agility, and reach of our small law firm was used to our advantage to achieve the considerable success that, until now, seems to have been monopolized by BigLaw – and in a fraction of the time.

We'll teach you how, with industriousness, strategic business acumen, and of course legal knowledge, we attained the success we desired in only a few short years – *not* decades. And while we build our firm, we thoroughly enjoy what we do. We have accumulated a deep bench of clients who we feel respect, like, and value us. We have arrived at a place where we can have the large office, the orchids in the lobby, and the impressive artwork, and *our* name on the door, all in a relatively short amount of time.

We came to believe that what was seemingly blocking us and other fellow lawyers from taking control and shaping our own practice were the myths that have grown out of the status quo of the BigLaw-dominated legal system. We felt that these myths served the BigLaw establishment by preserving its dominance in the industry by securing us as cogs in the system rather than enabling us to be contenders in the game. These myths appeared primed to keep us slogging through a steep hierarchy of positions, answering to others, with very few legitimate opportunities to obtain the security, lifestyle, prestige, and financial rewards that we were aiming for with our legal careers.

How do we know it's possible to build a phenomenally successful small, independent law firm? We know because we've done it. And from our experience, we've organized what we learned into what we believe is a replicable strategy and a set of tactics that you can learn and adopt in your own quest for legal career success and fulfilment. It took the rethinking of assumptions, the breaking of some taboos, and the refitting of approaches to suit a small, nimble firm so that we, too, could achieve what we believed to be the pinnacle of success in the legal profession.

"We" are Yussuf Aleem and Jacob Slowik, two young attorneys who have built a national, multi-million dollar per year practice representing an array of sophisticated clients with hundreds of millions of dollars in assets. We compete with some of the biggest law firms in the country and tackle many of the most high-profile matters within our niche business practice. We've got first class office space, a respected local and national reputation, and our own staff of associates. We've paid off our student debt, have the cars and homes of our dreams, and go on extraordinary vacations. We rarely have to work past an unreasonable time. We have time to devote to relationships, health, and fitness. We are published scholars and law school lecturers. And, yes, our names are on the front door.

In two short years, we accomplished our goals with minimal "traditional" legal experience, few connections and no monetary capital. We reached prestige and success equal to, or greater than, those of BigLaw partners. And we did so before we were 30 years old.

How did we so quickly accomplish what so many in the field don't even think is possible? Primarily by crafting a strategic and innovative approach to specialization in the legal field. By doing so, we were able to capitalize on certain tactics and outmaneuver the bigger, more established, and more rigid law firms. We hacked the system so that our smaller firm could succeed on its own terms.

From the start, we questioned the myths of BigLaw and challenged many of the sacred assumptions of the industry. In short, we thought for ourselves. We considered aspects of the business as any new entrepreneur would: from billing practices to staffing, from marketing to time management. We asked ourselves, *How do we build a profitable and sustainable law firm from where we are, not from where everyone said we needed to be?* And it worked.

We didn't have deep pockets to carry us, either. We built our multi-million dollar law firm from the ground up with very little in the way of capital contributions or monetary investment. Yet along the way (in two short years, remember) each of us has completely paid off our six-figure student loans and we are both in the envious position of being able to "retire" any time we want.

If you're skeptical, we're not surprised. After all, what we're saying flies in the face of the onslaught of legal academia brand messaging and BigLaw corporate marketing that you've consumed for years. Sure, the doubters will likely tell you that we are an exception to the rule and that aiming to create a multi-million dollar firm in a couple of years is a fantasy. They'll tell you we're an anomaly. They'll tell you that we got lucky. That we had the advantage of being Harvard Law grads and we happened to pick a once-in-a-generation niche that allowed us to finesse our way into a comfortable practice.

Our experience tells a different story.

The steps we took to establish a lucrative, sought-after, prestigious firm in two years largely consisted of eschewing the conventional wisdom of the legal profession and adopting a few flexible business practices that are simply more suitable for a new business fighting to take off. We capitalized on a strategic and innovative focus on business niche specialization. We broke a few once-sacred rules and thought more like businessmen than our legal education had trained us to. As a small "startup" law firm, we could afford to be more adaptable, so we worked smarter and implemented new approaches that ultimately benefited our clients as much as ourselves. We learned that consideration for scalability and financial responsibility plays a huge role in mitigating risk and maximizing opportunities. As a result, we've reached levels of success that most never attain.

At the same time, we are providing exceptional service to our clients; they, too, are winners in this bold adventure. This is the most important factor to which we attribute our success. Our clients get superior service, personal attention, and motivated attorneys. Plus, they pay significantly less than what the large firms would charge them. Ironic as it may be, successful attorney business practices don't have to be a win/lose scenario. You win; your clients can, and should, win, too. Our clients get from us what they frequently wished they had gotten from BigLaw.

If you're worried that you don't have the pedigree or background to do what we did, worry not. Based on our experience, the idea that you need the prestige of the "best" schools to enter the higher echelons of law practice is farcically overstated. The BigLaw-dominated "system" likes to perpetuate the perception that the most successful lawyers are those graduating from the highest-ranked law schools. That perception may serve their screening purposes, but it doesn't match our reality. Based on our experience, many lawyers who were top performers at small, non-prestigious law schools attain success within the legal industry. Perhaps it is because those from less renowned schools end up working harder and pursue legal career success in more "unconventional" ways. Despite the many examples of these individuals, the BigLaw partners obviously continue to rely on their firm's administration to actually do the hiring, and the administrators, owing to constraints on resources, cast their nets only at the top law schools. But we say fear not, graduates outside of the top-15! Our experience tells us there are many lawyers who have found success, both inside and outside BigLaw, without having graduated at the top of their class at a top-15 school.

Only rarely do our clients inquire about our scholastic background. When we sign clients, they typically do not know nor ask where we went to school. Our business pitch does not include a mention of the universities we attended. And from what we see around the country, there are quite a number of highly successful practices that are run by people who graduated from their local university law school, not an Ivy League campus. These lawyers did not need to come from a big name school to make a big name for themselves.

If you still have skeptics and naysayers insisting that you are mistaken to peel yourself away from BigLaw and set off in a direction of your own, we suggest that you consider their arguments thoughtfully, but also recognize their own personal bias, if any. We knew numerous colleagues who were frustrated and disillusioned, but still uncomfortable discarding their perceived safety and security in BigLaw. Yet they were also at that point in their lives somewhat invested in maintaining the status quo and averse to change. But we have found that change is now the norm and BigLaw is not immune. Skeptics predicted we would fall short of a sustainable practice. They could not have been more wrong.

We wrote this book to provide a blueprint for building a lucrative, distinguished, and sustainable private law practice of your own. To be sure, our success involved a lot of luck as well as a good deal of focused trial and error. But as a result of our efforts, we have distilled what we believe is a powerful formula that led to our success, a small law practice business strategy, and the tactics to support that strategy, which we believe may be replicable by those young lawyers with grit and willingness. We believe these guidelines can be adopted to increase your chance of realizing all the success you seek in your law career.

We recognize that everyone has their own starting place, a unique history, a different background story, and their own set of constraints and opportunities. But we firmly believe that your situation doesn't have to limit you. To succeed, we took advantage of opportunities that arose – opportunities that wouldn't have come to us if we had been chained to our desks day after day for the entirety of our careers. Yussuf took a leap by taking a job with a healthcare consulting company after only a year and a half in BigLaw, even though everyone warned him that it was too soon. Turns out it was precisely then that things started to happen and new opportunities presented themselves. It wasn't a rich relative, a professor friend at Harvard Law, or a connected classmate that made these opportunities for Yussuf. He made them for himself.

The experience and strategies in this book demonstrate how we sought out, recognized, and capitalized on opportunities when they appeared. These are the observations and lessons we would have provided to ourselves when we were starting out three years ago, the ones we would tell ourselves to follow. They can guide you to achieve success as a small law firm in just a few short years, as we did.

We'll show you how we chose the industry niche that's right for law firm success and helped us develop a robust legal expertise within that niche business, adopted flexible billing practices, and understood how marketing works for our law firm and strategy.

To begin with, we will show you we came to discard what we felt were the limiting myths and premises from the BigLaw-dominated legal career rulebook. We'll encourage you to think for yourself as you contemplate how to build a legal practice that brings you every one of the financial and personal rewards that you envision for your career in law. You just need to bring two things to the party: confidence in your own abilities and the willingness to figure out some things as you go along. Join us now as we show you how we built our own successful law firm and empowered our small law practice to make big money.

# 2. Our myths of the BigLaw system

In 2013, Yussuf was working as a junior associate at the Boston offices of Weil, Gotshal & Manges LLP. One morning, he learned that his firm had cut several jobs across the entire company. In fact, 77 people had been summarily fired – in one fell swoop – with no warning and no explanation. Some had been working there for only two months; others had been devoting endless hours of hard work for as many as seven years to the firm.[1] It didn't matter. Their jobs were gone. He was particularly struck by the situation of a colleague in his department. This young man, aged in his early thirties, had worked seven years at the firm. He had two young children. He had a mortgage and a wife who had stayed out of a formal job to take care of the children. He was still paying off student loans from law school. He was not equipped to go without work for very long, nor to take a roughly 50% pay cut, which is exactly what he would be facing. The exigency of his circumstances almost certainly meant a reduction in the quality of his next job.

We don't mean to pick on Weil Gotshal. They are a supremely talented group of lawyers delivering exceptional results for clients all over the world. Many people in the Boston offices had a tremendously positive impact on Yussuf and his early career. But what prompted these extreme cuts?

At the time, the law firm was not suffering in terms of their revenues, profits, or prestige. In fact, they were ranked ninth on the American Lawyer's A-List, which factors in metrics such as financial performance, pro bono work, associate satisfaction, and diversity.[2] They were earning over $2.2 million in profits per partner, raking in $1.2 billion in total revenues, and were rated sixth in

---

[1] https://dealbook.nytimes.com/2013/06/24/big-law-firm-to-cut-lawyers-and-some-partner-pay/

[2] https://www.law.com/americanlawyer/almID/1202793476168/

prestige according to the Vault rankings.[3] The actions that this one firm took are an example of where the interests of the largest, most successful law firms in the country truly lie, and give a clue about the reality of your future security if you work for them.

The perception of what we call *BigLaw* – a collection of the 150–250 most successful law firms in the United States who serve the country's largest corporations – has become a strategically generated, idealized vision of a benevolent career environment that has been effectively planted in our cultural imagination. Typically headquartered in the largest American cities, these firms often enjoy a major presence in New York, Washington, DC, Los Angeles, Chicago and San Francisco, with support offices in Europe, Asia and other continents. Partners at top BigLaw firms often generate incomes that most of us would aspire to.

At certain times, the status, the standing, and power of BigLaw were thrilling and intoxicating and we were driven to realize them for ourselves. But here's what we – and many others – have experienced: the aura of BigLaw is a veneer that's only skin-deep. It's as illusory as a magic trick. The marble floors, the immense staff, fancy skyscrapers, fresh orchids in the lobby, and the enormous artwork on the walls are not what they appear to be. The firms are simply not the bastion of security that we at one time perceived them to be.

To begin with, work in these law offices was against a backdrop of fierce competition, drudgery, dead-end jobs, unsatisfying pay levels and dwindling prospects for partnership. Our days were filled with long hours, competitive cultures, unrewarding work, and thankless tasks. You may feel the same, having sacrificed many of life's pleasures in the hopes of chasing your dream and securing a successful future. Early on in our time in BigLaw, we both faced a pressing question: will all of our hard work actually get us where we wanted to go?

The general story is by now well known and much analyzed. Prior to the Great Recession, BigLaw business was booming, along with the economy. Firms expanded and borrowed money to upgrade or enlarge their luxury offices. Others hired non-equity partners,

---

[3]   http://www.vault.com/blog/job-search/the-2013-vault-law-100-rankings-are-here

contract-based attorneys, and associates who were hoping to become partners, and offered them big salaries.

But when the international economy screeched to a halt in 2008, even the most prestigious and successful law firms were not immune to the fallout. Expansion was replaced by efforts to quickly contract, reduce, and streamline. Hiring of new associates came to a virtual standstill and more work got dumped on fewer and fewer associates. New employment opportunities diminished dramatically.[4]

Thankfully, the Great Recession is behind us. Now, the nation's unemployment rate is less than half what it was in 2009, consumer spending is up, and new startups of all kinds are booming – ripe with legal needs both corporate and litigious.[5] And given that the economy has recovered, we would expect BigLaw to once again return to its former status as a land of opportunity and a proving ground for the success track. But for us it hasn't. The hiring and firing practices that were brought on by the 2008 downturn are here to stay. BigLaw has become much more selective and much more efficient, and firms don't risk hiring more lawyers than they need. Large law firms are vigilant against the likelihood of another economic downturn, are remaining thinly staffed, and seem to be overworking employees quite intentionally so that they don't repeat the pain, risk, and loss of the era of the Great Recession. Additionally, we found that to apply to a position we found on LinkedIn for an attainable in-house job we would be competing against hundreds of other lawyers, a majority of whom inevitably had much more specialized experience than we had.

Since you're reading this book, you may well have been pounding the pavement for work and you're probably well aware of the fierce competition for legal jobs in today's world. While 83.7% of graduating law students in 2007 found positions requiring bar passage, within nine months of graduation, only 66% of 2016

---

4   See, https://www.nalp.org/2006entry-levelhiringatlawfirmsstrengthens, http://www.nalp.org/uploads/NatlSummChart_Classof2011.pdf; see also, https://www.law.com/nationallawjournal/almID/1202546791878/?germane=1202489565842&id=1202546791878

5   https://data.bls.gov/pdq/SurveyOutputServlet?request_action=wh&graph_name=LN_cpsbref3

graduates were in such a position.[6] In the past decade, 12 major firms – with 1000 partners between them – have collapsed entirely. It's a different world out there.

Also, if you happen to be of minority heritage, or female, your odds of finding the security and prestige that you think a job at BigLaw might bring are even worse. Despite progress in diversification in the past 10 years, women make up only 18.7% of equity partners and minorities make up only 6.1% of equity partners, according to a NALP survey among the NALP Directory of Legal Employers.[7]

In the meantime, law schools continue to attract prospective students as the notion persists that graduates' odds for employment are perennially bankable, that if students work hard, they can expect to find a satisfying, secure job waiting for them when they're done with their studies. But these misleading overtures are not without repercussions. Fifteen law schools across seven states have been sued for misrepresenting post-graduate career opportunities, including New York Law, Thomas Jefferson School of Law in California and San Francisco School of Law.[8]

But even if you are one of the lucky few to land a position at a BigLaw firm, the chances of getting a shot at becoming partner have never been lower. We saw that, while we waited for our ship to come in, we would likely suffer an often crushing workload, pressure to complete boring grunt work in record time, and last-minute emails demanding heroic efforts on time-sensitive assignments. We were expected to pick up our smartphone late into the evening no matter what we were doing or where we were. Many of our friends and classmates reported to us clocking virtually no time with any of the partners and a lack of attention to mentorship.

So we considered – is it all worth it? Going after the money, the prosperity, the success, and the dream? Of course it might be, if we had a reasonable chance of reaching those goals, and, at minimum, if we had a clear understanding of our odds and were willing to

---

    [6]   See, https://www.nalp.org/uploads/Class_of_2009_Selected_Findings.pdf; see also, https://www.nalp.org/uploads/1181_07selectedfindings.pdf
    [7]   https://www.nalp.org/0418research
    [8]   https://www.lawschooltransparency.com/blog/2011/10/15-more-aba-approved-law-schools-to-be-sued/

undertake the extreme sacrifices to get there. We mention this again – BigLaw may be just the right place for *you* to get your career started, if you can find a firm that fits your needs, and if you can make the needed connections and secure the necessary steps for advancement. With tenacity, resolve, patience, and sacrifice – some of the necessary characteristics of any lawyer who hopes to be successful – you might find your way to the top rungs of the ladder.

But of course when we were considering these things, we were extremely skeptical and thought, how reasonable *are* our chances?

## MYTH 1: ONCE WE GET OUR FOOT IN THE DOOR AT BIGLAW, OUR FUTURE IS SECURE

Money. Security. Prestige. These qualities define what success is for many young attorneys. They embody the reasons many work so hard for so long. They are the shiny objects that BigLaw dangled in front of our eyes as their confident recruiters and expert sales talks persuaded us that BigLaw was the best way to achieve them.

And of course we wanted those things! Who doesn't want to earn $180,000 right out of law school?[9] Who doesn't want to work in a high-class office, receive the respect of the profession, and be able to look forward to long-term job security? Who doesn't want to have the pleasure of sitting down at their Thanksgiving table and telling folks all about the "big deals" they've been working on? That is, if were able to leave our workstation to make it to the Thanksgiving dinner table.

There's nothing wrong with keeping a vision and working hard for it. But we found that we made some mistakes in our original perception of the security of BigLaw, the odds of attaining the highest level, and the brutality of the sacrifices that are necessary. Loyalty alone would not necessarily be rewarded.

Job security was one benefit that we expected from a career in BigLaw, but we found the promise of long-term stability a hollow one, simply because there are too many variables that come into play. For one thing, no matter where we worked, our career future would be subject to the numerous unforeseeable forces of the

---

[9]  When we started our careers, the entry salary at New York and Boston BigLaw firms was $160,000.

economy. Case in point: one BigLaw firm we knew of had a very busy, very large, and very lucrative bankruptcy department for many years. But from 2012 through 2016, when the fallout of the Great Recession finally began to subside, the number of major bankruptcies in the US fell to near zero. For two years, the firm did not receive a single bankruptcy case. There was no work. So they fired people. Layoffs and expendability became the new norm.

Imagine the bankruptcy associate who entered the firm one or two years before they downsized the department. Her training in filing bankruptcies was incomplete since she had only handled discrete and mundane tasks within a huge corporate bankruptcy case. She had no holistic view of how to run the process. If asked, she couldn't even file a bankruptcy for her neighbor. And now she's out of a job, and back at square one.

We have come to be wary of the optimist who claims layoffs are a thing of the past and structural adjustments mean that history will not repeat itself. Even if the economy continues to improve, even if you do get a job, you should always be suspicious about your job security at a big law firm. The aforementioned experience of Yussuf at Weil Gotshal remained seared into our brains. Top law firms just did not appear to be structured to be optimal for our legal careers. They did, however, seem to understaff their departments and overwork the well-intentioned, highly replaceable associates like ourselves for their benefit.

Meanwhile, we reasoned, following the Great Recession, corporate clients seemed more willing to betray loyalties than in the "good old days." The BigLaw firms could wake up any day to learn that one of their clients has fired them and hired someone else. When that happens, many of those firms need to fire an entire floor of associates. What do you think happened to the associates whose firm's "one or two" big clients included Lehman Brothers?

If you're at BigLaw now, think about the clients that your firm services. Chances are that a few big names keep coming up again and again. It's likely that one or two of them account for over half of the projects and assignments in your firm. What would happen if one of those big clients decided to reevaluate their relationship with your firm?

What would happen if the partner who is responsible for that big client relationship decided to re-evaluate their relationship with the law firm? Partners sometimes eye other options, seek greener grass, and ultimately make lateral moves. When they do, they often take their book of business with them to their new law firm. That means that if you're an associate, you could easily work for a couple of years in your department, even feel loyal to the partner you work with, only to one day find your job or at least your future advancement prospects have evaporated.

On the other hand, those partners who remain loyal often work into their 70s and 80s. We found that not all firms make a practice of forcing retirement. At the same time, more firms are recruiting partners from other firms to draw their clients with them. There's a boom in hiring non-equity partners and siphoning senior attorneys as "of-counsel" or "special counsel," instead of making them partners. Our conception of "security" was drastically altered upon seeing that the path upward was often a lateral one, and often involved the few true "rainmaking" partners.

We admit that these thought exercises are not the same as analyzing the big firm data, and are based largely on anecdotal observation, but we mention these considerations as this was part of our process in evaluating our career options, which eventually led us on our path to independent law practice and a successful small law strategy. We encourage you to at least ask these questions, and to investigate these matters on your own, with the abundant resources available.

If security drives you to BigLaw like it did for us, we invite you to challenge your perceptions, read between the lines and take a look behind the curtain. You may find that the safe, secure impression that BigLaw generates does not quite match the reality.

## MYTH 2: BIGLAW IS THE ONLY SURE PATH TO OUR FINANCIAL SUCCESS AND PRESTIGE

In years past, BigLaw starting salaries used to get bumped every couple of years or so; associates could count on their income matching the pace of the increase in cost of living.[10] But for the past 10 years, salaries have mostly stagnated. If you happen to live in a large city like New York, LA, or the Bay Area, and you have

---

[10]   https://www.nalp.org/1014research

the talent and connections, you just might be able to land an associate position with a cushy $180,000 starting salary. Yet with the cost of living being what it is in those metropoles, we found that our money did not go far at all. We were tempted to think that we were underpaid. However, upon considering the hundreds if not thousands of qualified lawyers who would kill for one of our BigLaw jobs, these starting salaries seemed to start making some sense again. On the other hand, outside a large city, a starting rate of $180,000 for a lawyer was unheard of. Even today, we are more likely to find a position at a smaller firm that offers to pay in the range of $75,000–$100,000 to start.

Is it prestigious to only see your children once a day – via Skype – while your spouse or nanny is getting them ready for bed? Is it prestigious to take out a loan to pay for your initial partnership interest, and then work 2200+ hour years for 8 years? Who's running whose world in this situation?

What sounds better to you: being one of thousands of BigLaw partners in one of the hundreds of large BigLaw firms, or being *the* top lawyer in clinical laboratory law in the entire United States?

Here's another way to look at it. A couple of mid-sized business clients that each earn a two-partner small law firm $2 million per year translates into $1 million profit per partner. That number will look even better when considering the number of hours going into producing such a figure.

Is that prosperous enough for you?

We found that with a few skills under our belts, a better than average understanding of law as it applies to a particular niche business, and the willingness to push through the early periods of building a business from scratch, we did not have to take a long time to build ourselves a very successful law practice. We got there quickly and have all the prestige that comes with being regarded as "go-to" specialists in a substantial business niche.

We refused to believe those who told us that we couldn't do what we set out to do. By most of the metrics we use to measure success – whether it's the amount of income, an impressive reputation, or the fancy office space – we found we can acquire all of that on our own terms in a reasonably short amount of time. Determined to work out of a fancy office building? We arrived there once we had purposefully and laboriously laid solid foundations for our practice. Want to work with high-powered clients? We now represent the same people that the best firms in the country fight to represent. Won't settle for an average salary? We take home incomes comparable with partners in BigLaw. Want prestige? Every evening, when we leave our class-A office space, walk past the receptionist desk, and travel down the elevator to our reserved parking spots, we know that we accomplished what we did without having a blueprint and as a result of our own trailblazing. We feel that we match, and in some ways surpass, the prestige and success attributed to BigLaw. We did it on our own. Our name is on the door. There's no feeling quite like it.

And we believe you can feel this way too.

## MYTH 3: STARTING A SMALL LAW PRACTICE IS TOO RISKY

Law schools and BigLaw contributed to the idea that starting our own law practice would be too risky and would not be able to provide us with job security. After all, the reasoning went, if we don't earn a paycheck, how will we be sure how much money we will make? How will we find clients? How will we know how to run the "business" of a law firm? How will we deal with a fear of running out of billable work and not being able to find more? Once we leave BigLaw, won't we be branded "burn-outs" and never be able to get a new job if things at our new independent firm go south?

But this myth of the riskiness of independent law practice does not reflect the reality. It seems to be merely a natural byproduct of BigLaw's incentive to perpetuate their dominance in the field of law. And when we took into account the time and effort we spent to make other people a lot of money, we needed to ask ourselves, and find out, if we could do it on our own.

By our very nature, we lawyers tend to be risk averse, so security is a sensitive issue. On the other hand, we can't overlook the fact there's at least some significant risk, even at BigLaw, as we identified by examining Myth #1. We also believe that any time anyone takes steps to reap potentially large rewards they will usually need to take some risks of some kind. The greater amount of risk is what enhances the reward, all else being equal.

However, we have come to believe that much of our perceived risk in starting an independent law practice has been founded on some misperception. Achieving success in a short amount of time was achieved by following the blueprint we lay out in this book. Becoming successful in our career took a lot of work. Building our independent law practice took time, strategic thinking, long-term planning, and adaptability to circumstances. It didn't happen overnight. We sacrificed. We had to empty the trash many nights. And if we had made different mistakes or behaved differently, and if the chips had fallen in a different direction, we may not have been here telling our story from a position of success. If you attempt to develop your own independent law practice, *you may fail.* But your destiny will be in your own hands. If you have the entrepreneurial spirit, that control is a kind of security that may be more rewarding for you in the long run.

Building an independent law practice and leaving behind a salaried position does involve a certain amount of risk. You might want to take a moment and consider what your risks actually are. That's how Jacob worked through his decision-making process. When Yussuf asked him to join forces in 2014, he thought to himself, '*Well, what do I really have to lose?*' At the end of the day, he figured, if all else failed, he still had his law degree and he could go and work for another firm. He could explain the decision to try to start a new firm. It sounded like a reasonable bet even to reasonable people who were enmeshed in a system that suggested otherwise. Assuming the worst, that the firm failed and he needed to seek a new job, he imagined having to explain the choice to a hiring partner at a new firm, and he saw that he could do it. His conclusion was that it was a risk worth taking.

On the other hand, everyone has a unique level of concern at stake; your risk profile might be quite different from Jacob's. You might be single, or you might have a spouse, two kids and a mortgage to pay. Your individual circumstances will – and should – influence the manner in which you take these bold steps. We encourage you to be honest with yourself about your circumstances in order to evaluate whether this is the right direction for you to go in.

As an independent firm, there are many ways that you can minimize your risks and respond efficiently to challenges. If the market demands it, we can adjust our rates. If business slows, we can evaluate and pursue the business development plans we think will be most fruitful. For a BigLaw associate, firm finances and overall performance are often a mysterious black box. Now that we run our own shop, we always know exactly where we stand, how lucrative are our prospects for future business, when a slowdown is likely, and more. We captain our own ship.

And we get to enjoy the rewards. As we pursued our goals, we knew with much better information and analysis when it would have been time to put a down payment on a new house or, instead, when it would have been time to pivot and dust off the resume for submission to other firms or in-house positions. We felt strongly that we should not be caught going into emergency forbearance on our mortgage because our firm unexpectedly made some long-term "adjustments," by eliminating our "secure" BigLaw positions.

We run our firm "lean." Scaling and financial responsibility play a huge role in mitigating risk. We did not start off in a fancy office building and with a huge staff, for example. We can also now negotiate fees more flexibly, as another example. In upcoming chapters, we'll go into more detail about how to make the most of every opportunity.

You can start planning now. If you're currently in a BigLaw job, for example, you can begin to set money aside to be able to adjust to an initial, temporary downturn in your income. Not all of your coffees or dinners are going to be covered by the client right away so don't buy that new Range Rover just yet. At the same time, begin to explore potential niche businesses in which you may be able to specialize – the subject of our next chapter.

You can share the risk. The partner(s), if any, that you choose to work with in your small law firm will also help you reduce risk by filling in the knowledge or skill gaps you need to provide the range of services your clients require. We got off to a quick start in large part because Yussuf excels with client development and possesses superior litigation skills, while Jacob came to master the nitty-gritty of operations and captained the transactional matters.

Worst-case scenario for us? Even if our small law practice did not succeed, there were still several options on the table for us. We could have attempted a return to BigLaw, wiser and more experienced, although to be sure there was no guarantee. BigLaw firms may have bristled to learn that we took matters into our own hands and had an independent spirit. Nevertheless, we could have sought to land at a regional large law firm, given that we accepted the prospect of having to be flexible with our choice of practice area and geographic location, in the event of our firm's failure. Firms do hire back people who have hung out their own shingle all the time. Yet all of those have failed before us probably have not benefited from the innovative strategies we describe in this book.

If you don't think you have a chance at BigLaw and you've even struggled to get regional law firm experience, the risk is even smaller for you. After all, you're not really giving up anything that promising or lucrative. You have less to lose and more to win.

Besides, the risk of self-starting a law practice is a different kind of risk that offers a greater amount of control and choice than BigLaw. You will be in control of the decisions that are made; you have a better ability to know the likely effects of those decisions; and when you implement them, you're more capable of being aware of the likely outcomes.

We reasoned that there's no more risk in launching our own law practice than any other independent business. We could argue that there's *less now for you* – because we've walked the path before you, taken note of where the pitfalls might be, and created maps you can now use to keep you moving forward. It may take some time for the money to accumulate at the rate you want, but if you're armed with the smart, strategic practices we offer here – we believe it will.

Who do you want to be making money for anyway?

## MYTH 4: WE NEED TO SPECIALIZE – AND BIGLAW IS THE BEST WAY FOR US TO DO SO

Law school taught us and our peers that to reach partner at a major law firm, we have to first establish an expertise in a particular field of substantive law and align ourselves with a practice specialty. Further, we learned that while schools traditionally offered general professional degrees in law, without requiring majors or concentrations, a number of law schools have shifted their curriculum recently toward more specialization. "Specialization" has attained buzzword status in numerous areas of the economy, and the legal profession is no exception.

Ironically, what comes along with our degree from law school is the warning that our narrow exposure to law means that we don't have what it takes to make it on our own out in the world. After all, the thinking goes, several highly specialized attorneys who knew nothing but credit default swaps probably lost their jobs in the 2008 financial meltdown and had to go back to square one to learn something else. These lawyers couldn't figure out how to leverage the expertise they had in the area that they had mastered, just as those lawyers who had become expert at bankruptcies were left high and dry when their firm laid them off.

Firm-wide attorney specialization is a major component to the BigLaw business model. As firms manage sophisticated, multi-billion dollar matters, they divvy up their work into logical categories in order to move forward and make an impact. Management organizes their business to maximize their efficiency and profits per partner. Their profit structure, designed around narrow bands of specialization, has been in place for quite some time.

That is exactly why we became wary of their insistence on funneling us and our colleagues into particular specialization silos. The firms appeared to be strongly, financially incentivized to do so and not so strongly incentivized to consider how that might impact our legal careers. BigLaw "specialization" is at least good for one thing – for enabling BigLaw to profitably handle very complex commercial transactions and litigations.

To be clear, we are not arguing that specialization is bad. In fact, it should not be avoided. But we came to adopt a different approach to specialization – an approach that put our career prosperity at the forefront. BigLaw did not help us specialize fast enough, in a niche or in a way that would enable us to be independent attorneys.

We infer that there are two major reasons that BigLaw wanted us to believe that narrow specialization is a necessary step to business growth. Most importantly, it has become a business technique to boost billings. Once a firm gets a large litigation or corporate matter in the door, they have five or six teams of specialized lawyers, all of whom will bill independently, at incredibly high rates, for their time. And they can tout that specialization as a justification for the high rates they charge.

Secondly, the BigLaw aura of specialization casts an impressive shadow simply as a marketing effort. It becomes a lucrative tool for self-promotion as they beat the drums of their areas of specialization and rank themselves against the performance at other firms. We saw that this dynamic was present with every new hire. As new associates came on board, fresh out of law school, they were taught to begin feeding the marketing machine right off the bat. A young recruit would be assigned to the corporate M&A team, Intellectual Property team, or something similar, and be told: 'This is the team you're working with. This is their specialty. And it's your job to market it as a specialty.' But let's get real: it's not their specialty. It's just the specialty of the team that has been assembled to more efficiently handle the discrete parts of one or several complex legal transactions. The individual associate's specialty could have been running document comparisons or making sure signature pages were in order and the correct number of copies were assembled for the closing sets of documents. The conventional wisdom seemed to attempt to persuade us that we needed to find a good specialization team in order to succeed in the firm and advance. That may have been true for a particular BigLaw firm, but it just wasn't so for our overall legal careers.

BigLaw forced us to think small about our individual legal practices. By limiting our focus, BigLaw served to influence us to believe that we didn't have what it took to maintain an independent practice. So we, and many of our classmates and colleagues, were dissuaded from even trying.

BigLaw's specialization tactics are fabulously successful for them – but seemed miserable for us. We are going to describe to you the business niche specialization strategy that we found far superior to any specialization that BigLaw tried to teach us. In Chapter 3, we will teach you how we mastered specialization for our small law practice. We'll identify the characteristics of our chosen business niche that we believe were fundamental to maximizing our chances of success with our independent law practice. Whether it may be delivery drones, tele-medicine kiosk franchises, social network data security and portability, or some other emerging niche, we'll identify the characteristics of a business niche on which we focused and which will help you to pick a niche for which you have an affinity and that you can leverage to attract and sustain paying, loyal clients. In the remaining chapters, we will discuss several tactics we used to construct a sustainable and attractive practice around our chosen business niche.

Understand that a specialty does not, in fact, have to limit you. In many situations, our fledgling firm was better served by our willingness to take on a matter outside of our "traditional" legal skill specialties. Limiting ourselves to one type of legal transaction may have served BigLaw's competitive strategy quite well, but we found that it was unnecessary and even was limiting to our path to career fulfilment. When clients come to us with needs that fall somewhat outside the scope of our experience, we still determine how we can best offer to help. We're upfront with them about any limitations and let them know we are happy to take the time to figure out what is necessary to achieve a superior client result. Having established a track record of excellence and having earned their trust, our clients are usually happy to give us the green light to move forward with an issue. As a result, we expand our field of expertise while providing excellent service to our clients at a more comfortable price point for them. And they don't have to go shopping around for and vetting another set of lawyers.

If you don't have the time or inclination to delve into the law governing a new business niche, you can also still keep it in-house by teaming up with other attorneys and learn from them as you go. Many of our clients become very attached to us as their lawyers and feel more comfortable if we are involved, even if we're not the lead in the matter. They let us act as a liaison with a specialist in the area of law at issue and they want us to supervise the case so we can be there for them, inform, and reassure them. With this approach, we deepen and expand our relationship with our client, while learning about the new field in the process. In the meantime, we've also broadened our expertise. Specialization should be taken in a manner that benefits your career, first and foremost, not the profits of the partners for whom you work in your first job out of law school.

So let's get started. In the next chapter, we'll share with you our secret sauce of hacking the traditional legal career path so quickly and so successfully – business niche specialization.

# 3. Business niche specialization

In April 2017, our firm participated as exhibitors in the American Telemedicine Association's Telehealth 2.0 Conference in Orlando, Florida. The annual conference is the leading event in the tele-medicine industry, an area of law that we were investigating and were interested in pursuing. We had done our homework research-ing emerging business models within this industry and we had actually already successfully represented a few clients in tele-medicine business transactions. Our experience and research en-abled us to speak credibly as a law firm with a well-founded grasp of the industry and an ability to guide clients and their businesses through the unique complexities of the tele-medicine industry.

As exhibitors, we provided marketing materials that highlighted our experience with tele-medicine transactions and presented talk-ing points that would be pertinent to any business interested in, or based on, tele-medicine. We came with the focused intention to stand out from the other law firms at the conference and to get the attention (and business) of lucrative clients in this rapidly emerging multi-billion dollar sub-industry within healthcare.

There were thousands of attendees comprising hundreds of businesses operating and innovating in this rapidly expanding tele-medicine niche. We had identified tele-medicine as a niche that is well-suited to our firm's growth strategy. To start, it was a rapidly growing industry and its market share was not (at least not yet) dominated by a few major companies. Telemedicine providers were already generating significant revenue from reimbursements from health insurance companies and direct payments from providers, so they were profitable enough to be able to pay law firms for their services. Also, since tele-medicine operates within American healthcare, its extensive regulations continue to evolve, creating a lot of legal gray area to be navigated by these cutting-edge companies.

To our surprise, we were the only law firm that bothered to set up an exhibit at the conference, so every attendee, exhibitor, and speaker with any type of legal question – no matter how abstract or tangential to tele-medicine – found their way to our booth, and our booth alone, to get their legal questions answered.

In the waning hours of the day, one of the conference speakers, a lawyer at a BigLaw firm who had dedicated most of his practice to tele-medicine over the past few years, approached us. For quite a while we were engaged in lively conversation about the state of the industry, regulatory and legal trends, and the promising companies in attendance. Before he left, he looked at us one more time and shook his head. He confessed that he admired our approach and wished he had thought of it himself.

Because of our attendance at that conference, we were hired by three new major clients. One was a major eyewear company that wanted to offer eye exams and prescriptions via tele-medicine. Another was a large network of hospitals looking to integrate with tele-medicine providers. The other was a foreign company looking to partner with American healthcare providers in order to offer its tele-medicine platform.

Why was our experiment such a success? We researched it well, saw the potential, and presented ourselves as authoritative experts in the legal issues of the industry. At that moment, we could easily have been considered one of the top five or 10 tele-medicine law firms in the nation, based on our demonstrated knowledge and consideration of tele-health business, if not experience. Owing to our strategy and our efforts, we accrued a significant clientele in a relatively short period of time.

So why didn't any BigLaw firm care to show up and demonstrate – to potential clients with billions of dollars to invest – that they were making efforts to stay ahead of the curve with this emerging industry? The answer is that they had not identified the tele-medicine industry as a target market. It was already now one of ours.

This anecdote highlights the fundamental strategy that we believe has been the most important component of our model for success for our law firm: *business niche specialization*. It's a strategy that we have come to believe, through our experience, is better suited to the size, agility, reach, and advantages of our smaller, independent firm than any other models we have seen and/or experimented with ourselves. As this strategy has served remarkably well for us, we believe that business niche specialization can provide a smart lawyer with a path to the kind of income and/or prestige one would expect as a partner at a large firm – in a fraction of the time. And it's the key ingredient to our "secret sauce" that allowed us to build a million-dollar law practice so quickly and so successfully.

We saw first-hand that for many partners at BigLaw firms, their business objectives appeared to be primarily about capturing engagements with the top corporations in the world. They spent resources in hopes of landing the legal business of the Fortune 500s, in order to bring in the revenues that would generate profits for partners at the level they sought. In fact, owing to the size of the BigLaw firms, and the number of partners they support, many focus mainly on going after the proverbial "biggest fish" in order to support operations, overhead, and profit structures.

Just as much as BigLaw needs those large, multinational corporations to stay on top, those corporations need BigLaw firms to serve them. After all, their needs are great: they have highly complex, rapidly emergent legal issues and an endless number of people whose job it is to deal with them. Fortune 500s need BigLaw firms to answer every legal query, look into every variety of issue that comes up on a daily basis, and have the answers for every type of transaction that is of concern – and do it 24 hours a day, 7 days a week, 365 days a year. If you've worked in BigLaw, you know the feeling of keeping your phone's email alert on loud even when you go to sleep. You know the feeling of spending Thanksgiving around a closing table for one of the clients' major deals.

But as we launched our small independent law firm, it seemed that we were not in the position to compete with BigLaw for that business market. We didn't have the resources, the reach, or the background to provide the entire array of services that BigLaw does. But that was okay. There has been plenty of work to be secured (and money to be made) – just as high profit margins per partner – for our small law firm by going after mid-size companies within a particular business niche – a niche possessing certain characteristics making it ripe for anchoring and supporting a profitable law firm. These companies needed competent, proficient, smart, educated lawyers to help them with their legal needs, too.

They demonstrated time and again that wanted lawyers who understood their business, first and foremost. And they paid well for such lawyers. We made this type of niche and these mid-sized companies our target market.

When CEOs of the small to mid-level companies whom we represented were forced to deal with legal matters, they typically didn't have the resources or inclination to decide between calling a litigation lawyer, a corporate lawyer, or a tax lawyer. He or she wanted to have one lawyer's phone number who knew their business well and who could take care of any and all of their legal matters one way or the other. Even if the lawyer didn't have all of the answers right there and then, he's the one who will be most efficient at figuring out every single aspect of the transaction in question.

For example, imagine you operate a small medical laboratory (a laboratory performing genetics, toxicology and pathology tests for patients referred by physicians, hospitals and other medical providers) and you have legal concerns. You want to find a lawyer who knows the business and legal issues of medical laboratories. Your laboratory has been around for a year, has positive cash flow and some solid groups of referring providers, but is by no means a dominant player. You don't particularly want someone who is generally considered an "all-purpose" healthcare lawyer with limited laboratory-specific experience, who you'd have to pay, in effect, to learn to become a medical laboratory lawyer. It's more efficient for you to go to the medical laboratory industry expert first.

The attorney with experience working with medical laboratories appreciates the specific business concerns of these types of clients and does not come with a mind laser-focused only on black letter legal issues of limited practical application. The laboratory lawyer comes already equipped with the education they need to serve you, and in which they've already invested their own time and money to help your business specifically. Most likely, they've already asked the critical legal questions that you are asking, and they've asked those questions from the perspective of a peer laboratory, not an entirely different business like, say, a hospital, an urgent care clinic, or a solo doctor's office. Whereas an "all-purpose" healthcare lawyer might have been limited as such, the laboratory lawyer understands how your laboratory operates, how you make money, and what your diverse products and services are. They are aware of most of the regulations which apply to your operation, and, more importantly, they are aware of which regulations are the hardest for laboratories to follow and the ones most frequently implicated in laboratory day-to-day operations. They are familiar with the unique factors that differentiate the laws that are applicable to the transactions that pertain to your laboratory and the industry trends for the laboratory industry. Having that knowledge makes the laboratory lawyer the expert that laboratory CEOs want to be able to pick up the phone and call.

As an independent firm specializing in this particular business niche, we became the lawyers these clients call. We had not spent 25 years litigating and we had not seen every type, variety or flavor of corporate transaction. We were not credentialed as tax law experts. But we had the depth of understanding of the medical laboratory CEO's business better than all three of those hypothetical other lawyers put together. And we had the flexibility to make sure any of these things got done well for the client, in the most efficient way possible.

Business niche specialization means to become a go-to legal specialist for a particular business niche possessing the knowledge and ability to handle a variety of legal maneuvers and transactions that are specific to the business niche. With an exceptional business niche, and if done right, we believe the business niche specialization strategy can provide the accelerated track to success as a small law firm which it provided for us. After all, a small, independent firm won't have the astronomical revenue requirements that BigLaw firms carry. Do the math. If a firm with 400 partners wants to make $1 million per partner, they'll need to rake in $400 million in profits every year. And they'll need a lot of clients with lucrative work to bring in that kind of profit.

But if you're a small firm comprising two partners and you want to make $1 million each, you need to bring in $2 million in profits. And you can do it with much lower costs. And by choosing the right business niche, you will only need a handful of clients to get you there.

## OUR STORY

Here's how we discovered – and leveraged – the power of business niche specialization and turned it into a multi-million dollar annual revenue law firm business.

We (Yussuf and Jacob) originally met as classmates at Harvard Law School. We stayed in Cambridge after graduation and studied for the bar exam together. Thankfully, we did not want to kill each other after that experience, although there may have been some tense moments after days of reviewing outlines and listening to Barbri lectures at 1.75× speed. Both of us immediately took jobs at BigLaw firms. Yussuf went to a large firm in Boston that specializes in private equity and Jacob went to a firm in New York and joined their top-rated commercial real estate department.

After about two years in Boston, Yussuf took a leap of faith and moved to Atlanta, Georgia after accepting a job as general counsel for a startup laboratory consulting company. The company helped laboratories in a variety of ways and usually as part of a "turn-key" development solution. They helped develop their infrastructure, brought in equipment, recruited and hired employees, set up billing systems, and sometimes even did the billing for them. In the course of his work as general counsel for the company, Yussuf met with many clients in the laboratory industry, from those who had already launched mid-size laboratories to those who were in the early stages of developing their own new laboratories. Time and again, over half of the conversations focused on legal questions; and everybody needed to ask Yussuf for the answers. By necessity, Yussuf dove into the extensive research and work that was required to disentangle the clients' various real-world legal issues. At an accelerated pace, he accumulated a far-reaching, in-depth, and rare education in laboratory law.

Yussuf spoke to senior healthcare attorneys, partners at large, prestigious law firms, and achieved a mastery of the subject matter beyond the often generalized, survey-level understanding of those he spoke to. Those "big-time" healthcare partners were plenty comfortable to simply hear the laboratory's, or potential laboratory's, situation, spot some issues, and say "No," to most, if not all, of their proposals, while billing thousands of dollars for a 10-page memo to issue their "No" answer. On the other hand, Yussuf might say "No," too, but then he would offer alternatives and hold countless conversations to understand the nuance of the issues. He took the time to get a deeper grasp of the statutes, regulations, guidance, enforcement actions, commentary and opinion, and to chart a path to a "Yes" that was palatable to the business and legal risk considerations of the client.

It soon dawned on Yussuf that his unique expertise was a viable avenue to a standalone practice. He was mastering the law in a lucrative business niche. So Yussuf spoke to the consulting company and came to an agreement in which he'd leave their employment and set up with an independent law practice. He would be free to bring in his own new clients and enhance his own laboratory niche expertise by handling more and different matters and clients at different points in their business life cycle. And he eventually asked Jacob to join him in this new venture to grow the institutional capacity of the law firm.

We hit the ground running. We poured through books on Medicare law and healthcare regulations, and read every article we could get our hands on that pertained to the business of laboratories and ancillary healthcare providers. We reviewed cases and argued both sides back and forth with each other. We investigated reports on legal issues of laboratory law in industry blogs. Eventually, the firm added a few clients, one with a multi-million dollar lawsuit with a competitor alleging theft of trade secrets, tortious interference, and illegal solicitation of clients and employees. With each task and each case, we grew as clinical laboratory attorneys and word-of-mouth began to build. We made more connections. We represented another laboratory that was fighting a lawsuit with another laboratory. After the suit was resolved, the other laboratory – the one to whom we had previously been averse – eventually signed on as a new client for a new commercial transaction. They hired us based on our already demonstrated expertise and intimate knowledge of both the legal issues and unique business considerations. In other words, we knew their business much more than their own lawyers did. And while we would maintain that our legal acumen was also greater, this wasn't necessarily the metric that motivated that client to go with us. They valued our specific medical laboratory experience.

This was an important lesson, which we will unpack throughout this book. Consulting companies recommended us to laboratories.

Sales folks recommended us to friends who worked in sales at other laboratories. Billing companies recommended us. And business took off.

We learned the industry. We were taking calls for certain legal issues, transactions, and occurrences that we had never handled before, but we knew the laboratory's perspective inside and out so we could research and unpack the issues and advise the clients well. We knew what their goals and objectives were, and we had the legal skills to come up with all of the relevant information and help counsel the laboratories to make decisions in the best way in view of the often novel legal issues in play.

At first, we took on some limited matters at or below cost. Sometimes laboratories would come to us with very specific regulatory questions that were unique to their operations and to them. They just wanted a single question answered. By taking those first few assignments below cost we demonstrated our expertise, reliability, and professionalism. At the same time, we learned another lesson – that it can be tricky to compete with other law firms based on cost alone. But soon enough, those cases led to more substantive and more lucrative work, like large-scale litigations, audits with Medicare and private insurance companies, financings and sales, acquisitions and general expansion.

While we became experts in our business niche, we spent no time plotting how to go after LabCorp or Quest, the two largest clinical laboratory companies in the US at the time, each with hundreds of millions of dollars in revenues annually. Together, by some measures, we believe they comprise greater than one-half of the entire clinical laboratory industry market. We left them alone and went after their mid-sized regional competitors. In the process, we quickly made a name for ourselves and have now become one of the go-to laboratory law firms in the United States, with over 20 laboratories on our client roster.

## RETHINKING SPECIALIZATION

As we've discussed, the specialization track for an attorney in a BigLaw job is driven more by the business interests of the firm than concern for individual attorneys' long-term career development. The BigLaw firms will have attorneys "specialize" in an area that most suits their needs for the foreseeable future – not necessarily the attorney's foreseeable future. Specializing in corporate bankruptcy law for the first seven years of your career, for example, will fulfill the needs of a BigLaw firm because they need you to do just that. But after those seven long years, they won't necessarily make you partner; in fact, they might just kindly ask you to "transition" from the firm. Meanwhile, for those seven years of your life, you haven't learned enough about any particular niche to make you a true specialist. Remember the corporate bankruptcy attorneys who lost their jobs when the number of corporate bankruptcies throughout the country fell to almost nothing? And the securitization attorneys specializing in credit default swaps who lost their less-than-secure jobs during the credit crisis? Exactly our point.

On the other hand, as a solo or small independent firm, strategically using specialization to set you apart can springboard you to the top. You need to learn how to pay attention to the benefits of specialization if you want to do it successfully.

Let's look a little closer at what we mean when we talk about specialization. Ever more forces are increasing the push for specialization as it has become a highly valuable business tactic in countless industries. Increasing globalization, increasing legal and regulatory complexity, ever-evolving technologies, and an expert-driven economy are all contributing to the desire of consumers to seek out specialists in more narrowly defined areas. Chances are you took an economics course in college where you had an introductory explanation of the economic principles underlying the benefits of specialization. Perhaps you were exposed to a mathematical representation of those benefits and how they add up in a few specific and/or hypothetical situations. Kudos to you if you retained enough of those lessons that you could explain the concepts to an uninformed person. For our purposes, let's assume you acknowledge that there are benefits to specialization. Then, where do you go from there? How much specialization? What type of specialization? How early in your career should you focus on trying to specialize? How do you know you're picking the right specialization?

Law schools seemed to only focus on guiding students into the most general entry into specialization and gave us very few further clues besides telling us to pick between corporate law or litigation. It seems to work for the law schools because they don't have to do any more than that to continue to get the hundreds of thousands of school applicants they get every year. So, we have found that we rarely find someone in law school who says they want to be a lawyer for a specific business niche, say, a new drone technology company, for example. Yet we believe such a person has the key to potentially achieving just as much success in their legal career as any BigLaw partner – and in much less time.

BigLaw guided us to focus on legal skills like litigation or corporate law, but for us, we reasoned that those will probably not be optimal for our long-term career prospects based on our interests and how we envisioned a fulfilling legal career. Besides, legal skills like litigation or corporate law are the broadest forms of specialization: they are the least specific and offer no defined expertise. They focus on the skill, not the specialty. Narrowing it down by industry – finance, oil and gas, healthcare – does help refine a specialty further. Beyond that, identifying the type of transactions – like mergers and acquisitions, financing, and divorce – provides a slightly greater degree of specialization. But we believe the best level of differentiation is the business niche.

For example, when an attorney says she's a healthcare lawyer, what exactly does she mean? She could be a novice doing almost anything in an increasingly vast and complex industry. Perhaps she's a litigation associate at a BigLaw company and the two major cases she worked on in her entire five years there were pharma trade secret cases. Maybe she's done employment disputes for healthcare companies like hospitals, physicians, or pharma companies. Or possibly she has done Health Insurance Portability and Accountability Act (HIPAA) work for a large healthcare software company.

But she might not know how important trade secret protection is to clinical laboratories. She may not know how HIPAA impacts a large independent ancillary services provider, she might not be capable of helping with non-HIPAA-related regulations, and might not be equipped to perform transactional work because she's only done litigation and administrative law matters. There are thousands of healthcare lawyers out there just like her, with only a slight specialization in their practice, specialization focused on a legal skill rather than a business niche, and thus lacking the critical ingredients to which we attribute our success as an independent law practice.

But when we say we're clinical laboratory lawyers, we've identified ourselves as one of a very small number of attorneys who have mastered that territory. And we've put ourselves in a position to be highly sought-after, highly paid specialists within our chosen business niche.

Once we found the right business niche to specialize in, we found that we were in a unique position to attract new business with appealing pricing policies. This is especially important in today's financial environment where competition is intense, and low-cost offers are everywhere. It used to be that lawyers could only survive by charging high prices for work that would often require quite a few tasks that were fairly easy to produce, while the more challenging work was sprinkled in the mix. But with technology and information literally at almost everyone's fingertips these days, many legal tasks that used to be the sole territory of lawyers can be accomplished by almost anyone with access to a computer or mobile device.

We're not proposing a get-rich-quick scheme here. We still had to work hard and do the substantive work that our clients needed in order for us to achieve the kind of success we were seeking. Anyone attempting to follow our blueprint is in for countless challenges requiring grit and hard work. It will necessarily involve complicated legal work so you will need to spend a lot of time reading and analyzing complex and sometimes novel legal issues. However, the key takeaway is that this toil had a greater return on investment for *our* career compared with similar toiling in BigLaw. Our work propelled us to a mastery of the legal issues in a business niche in which we could set ourselves apart and generate business for ourselves independent of the BigLaw model. And by modeling our business this way, we were able to achieve that success in a fraction of the time that most partners in BigLaw do.

Specialization within a business niche puts you in the enviable position of capturing higher margins in the long run. Below, we'll discuss our particular business niche for the purpose of identifying key characteristics of business niches that we believe underscored our ability to build a successful practice within that niche. These characteristics should be used to analyze potential business niches on which you are considering focusing for the purpose of starting your independent law practice.

Our beliefs on what make a good business niche for starting a law practice by no means reduce to a rigid formula and these characteristics do not produce a magic bullet for success. Not all niches are created equal and not all lawyers are created with the full capabilities of turning an otherwise promising niche into a successful law specialization. In other words, this strategy is not for all lawyers. In fact, it's not for most lawyers.

Even if you have read the rest of this book, have done your research and found what you believe is a promising niche, but still have some doubt or uncertainty about the niche you choose, you won't find out unless you try. We have all heard and probably have experienced to some degree that lawyers are naturally more risk averse than the general population. Here's where you need to fight that tendency. Of course you might wonder if any particular niche is the "correct" one for your success. Or you might wonder if you will truly enjoy working within a particular business niche or whether some other sexy niche over there might be better to try like that one that's exploding in some other sector altogether. Here's where it's important to trust your judgment to identify the characteristics we describe below and to pick a niche that has some potential. If it does not work out right away you always have options to try new niches, but you will not find out anything by continuing down your current, same path. This is one situation where risk-taking tends to work well.

In later chapters, we'll discuss how we better organized our business to suit our smaller footprint and how we used strategic business tactics most effectively. But the advantages we gained by selecting and working within a lucrative business niche cannot be overstated.

## QUALITIES OF OUR LUCRATIVE BUSINESS NICHE

Selecting a worthy business niche to specialize in turned out to be the most important step we took in the operation of our firm. We picked well, and because of that, we avoided the expense, time, and frustration of having to regroup and pivot several times down the road until we struck a niche that works.

How do you determine which business niche is a good one to build your law practice around?

Now that our business niche strategy has crystalized with medical laboratories and since we have continued to experience steady success with such a strategy, we have determined that there are five fundamental factors to qualify a business niche as a lucrative one. The five characteristics associated with a lucrative small law business niche are, in no particular order:

- emerging
- profitable
- mid-sized
- complex
- in early stages of development.

We believe that when all of these factors are present in a business niche, a new firm will predictably grow quickly, dependably, and profitably. Let's go over them one by one.

**Emerging Business**

First, we believe that it was crucially important that our business niche was an emerging one, where the number of new entrants in the specific area or industry was increasing. When we started out, clinical laboratories were a growing niche within the healthcare industry, there were more and more laboratories opening all of the time, and we were well positioned to grow right along with it. Sometimes it's not very obvious that an industry is growing. Maybe there aren't many other lawyers specializing in it, for example. But that would also signify less competition and fewer barriers to entry to that niche. On the other hand, some businesses aren't so much emerging as they are receiving increasing attention at a given time. The difference is that emerging industries have a longer-term outlook than that. They have a growth trajectory that is undeniable. They're the ones that you want to get into at the ground floor, if possible, so that when they rise, you rise with them.

**Profitable Business**

Second, our niche consisted of plenty of individual companies that were already profitable, enough so that they could reliably pay for attorneys. We were taking enough risk already by forming an independent law practice; we did not want to multiply the risk factor of our endeavor by also adopting the risk underlying that business niche. In other words, we did not find ourselves in a position where we were saying, "*If* this industry becomes profitable, we will find success and make a lot of money as the expert attorneys." Profitable companies pay for lawyers. Period. We thrived representing clinical laboratories in part because they were quickly profitable: within the first three months of opening, new laboratories were showing a profit and were able to pay their consultants and lawyers. On the other hand, startup app companies or companies doing space exploration may not be a good choice of business niche on which to anchor a law practice. They're not going to want to pay lawyers if they don't have to. The paying of legal bills is always under scrutiny by investors who are impatiently waiting to recoup or realize an exit.

**Mid-Sized Participants**

The third important factor for our niche was the size of the companies in the industry. As we've mentioned previously, we did not spend any time trying to score business from Quest or LabCorp, the two largest companies within the medical laboratory niche at the time. We also did not grow to be a million dollar law practice by representing very small local laboratories. To be more specific to our niche, some solo physician and/or small medical practices wholly own and operate their own laboratories, and they most often do not accept test referrals from outside of their practice. These can be generally considered the smallest participants in the laboratory industry. They certainly have legal issues, but once they get up and running, these small practices, by necessity, tend to keep the legal issues, and thus the legal spending, to a minimum. While we did represent some of these small "physician-owned" laboratories, we did not stake the success of our firm on the revenue generated by the work from these small entities. We probably could survive on such business, but would not have grown to achieve the success that we sought. Thankfully the laboratory industry was rich with so-called "mid-sized" companies. These laboratories were often focused on a specific region within the United States, say, the southeast. They were referred tests by several dozen or even hundreds of medical practices, but perhaps not thousands. They focused on forging solid relationships with medical practices based on attempting to provide superior customer service. Individually, they did not threaten the industry dominance of the big players. They may have offered a dozen laboratory tests rather than thousands of different tests. They may have kept their sales force lean and focused on only very efficient tests or customers who generated predictable levels of referrals. Nevertheless, these laboratories were able to generate millions of dollars in revenue. And there were dozens of these "mid-sized" laboratories.

We believe that a good business niche will exist within an industry with a robust "middle class." So we may not consider a smart phone manufacturer, a social network like Facebook, or other mega-industry. We consider the ones with lots of participants that manage on the order of millions of dollars, not billions of dollars, in revenue. There are thriving players who occupy less than 50% of market share or make up a good chunk of a less-than-50% market share. This dynamic might be found in a variety of niches. Sometimes they are suppliers, sometimes they have regional advantages, sometimes they have new technology advantages. Laboratories have advantages in regions and have advantages with a particular technology, such as a new type of test, or advantages based on contracts with big clients like hospital systems or even governments. What is key is that the middle players are profitable and lucrative enough to support a healthy market for legal services.

**Legal/Regulatory Complexity**

The fourth factor that made our business niche lucrative is that it had a high degree of operational and legal/regulatory complexity at the time. The laws pertaining to laboratory operations and regulations are complex and often subjective to the matter. We believe that if most of the legal issues facing laboratories were black and white, then any established lawyer could just as easily have given our clients a satisfactory answer as an "expert" laboratory lawyer. But because medical laboratories consistently operate in an industry and regulatory scheme with a lot of legal "gray area," then knowing the business and being a business expert proved to have outsize value for our clients, and thus legitimized the value of our focused experience and knowledge. The clients needed adept help to know how to navigate those gray areas around their particular business and industry.

When it comes to asking what you need to do to buy a building, for example, the answers are fairly easy to come by. Buildings have been bought and sold in this country for hundreds of years and the folks building businesses out of developing these buildings have been doing so for hundreds of years. Yes, there may be new regulations to deal with or weird circumstances that arise as the world changes, but we already know 99% of what we'll likely encounter in the transactions pertaining to buying a building. Further, there are thousands of lawyers in every city ready to figure out that 1% of new complexity.

We observe that we flipped that dynamic: we found a niche where we were the 1% of lawyers trying to figure out something closer to the 99% of the unknown, unsettled legal and regulatory complexity. The answers to questions about how to legally operate a compliant clinical laboratory are filled with gray areas, conditionals, what ifs, unapplied or unsettled standards – they are intricate, subjective, and have lots of nuance. We like to say that if you give us half a day examining any laboratory, we will find a handful of technical violations of some law, rule, or regulation. (Of course, this doesn't apply to our own clients!) For that reason, laboratories needed the attention of an attorney with experience and proficiency in the industry to unravel and adequately comply. Regulation-heavy businesses are great examples of businesses with this characteristic.

**Early Stages of Development**

Lastly, a well-picked niche is an area of law that is still in development. Industries like drones and tele-medicine have just gotten started and the areas of law pertaining to them are in their infancy. That means that you can grow quickly from novice to expert because the law is so new and hasn't been fully formed. That 99% of complexity is actually growing just as fast, if not faster, than it is being settled. The rate at which the gray area issues arise is growing. This may be due to rapidly changing technology but, in the case of laboratories, it is mostly due to frequently changing regulations.

For better or worse, nearly every new presidential administration seems to attempt to "solve" healthcare without adequately judging the success of the efforts of prior administrations or without an accurate assessment of what is working or not working in the current scheme. Mix in the effects of politics, and we find that every administration is only reliably successful in creating more gray areas of regulation that require lawyers to help navigate, help decide, and challenge if necessary. Contrast that with the real estate industry, where almost every conceivable quirk of a real estate deal has happened, has been litigated, and has been decided in a US court of law. Real estate has a saturated market of specialists. That wouldn't have served us as well as our laboratory niche. If the area of law you're considering is still fairly uncharted, there won't be very many experts already in the field yet, so it will be faster and easier for you to set yourself apart and make an impact.

Let's see how our factors apply to particular industries. Healthcare law, for example, does qualify as a profitable and growing industry, and its area of law is complex, but healthcare law is not a specialized business niche, so it would not be an optimal area on which to focus a small independent law firm. Do a Google search for "healthcare lawyer" and you'll see what we mean. You'll probably find hundreds of listings for attorneys just in your city alone. Now try to Google "laboratory attorney." You'll probably find only a handful in the entire country to match the description. That's the positioning that business niche specialization can get you.

Many attorneys who attempt to open small, independent law practices begin with the idea of focusing on "startup law" or law typically focusing on new technology or software companies like a Facebook or a Dropbox. While these efforts are increasingly popular, startup law violates some of the criteria we have for being a good bet as a business niche. Why? Startups, in general, are frequently not profitable. They don't necessarily have gray areas of legal considerations, and they are not a business niche in and of themselves. However, you could look to represent a business or type of business that works *for* startups, like VCs focusing on a particular niche of investments (the autonomous vehicle segment, for example), data security consultants, or data security technology companies. Any of these could lead to a promising niche law practice. If you only seek startups as clients because everyone seems to be talking about them, then you'll very likely struggle to gain traction and you'll be at the mercy of competition from everywhere – including established BigLaw firms.

Ironically, if you like the type of issues, the challenges, and even the clients that you experience working with startup businesses, then you're especially suited to following our track to success. When you select a business niche that follows the principles we describe in this book, you'll probably be doing a lot of work for startups, as we did when we started out. You can pick a business niche and find a subset of startups within that niche.

Being a small law firm put us in the enviable position of being able to select an area to specialize in that works for us, not against us. We are in the unique position to be able to provide a depth of research in our chosen area of law, and that gives us an expertise that others will seek out and for which they pay well. The characteristics outlined above – business niches that are on a growth trajectory, clearly profitable, appropriately sized, complex with lots of gray area, and enjoy a demand for definition and refinement – were the key factors of our business niche specialization strategy that we believe allowed us to minimize risk and maximize the potential profitability in our small firm.

Areas of law such as tele-medicine, drones, data protection software, and e-sports are just a few of the many business niches out there that will very likely serve as a good niche to begin to investigate and which may serve to put you on the fast-track to million-dollar revenues as a small, independent law firm.

## THE IMPORTANCE OF LEGAL SKILL DIVERSITY

Contrary to the prevailing wisdom (and inertia) of law schools and BigLaw, while business niche specialization is the fundamental key to hacking the legal profession in favor of your career, we also found it necessary to have a diversity of legal skills to handle the breadth of work our clients needed. They asked us a variety of legal skill questions and we needed to be able to answer them. Maybe there's a lawsuit. Maybe they have a dispute with an employee or executive. Maybe they want to buy or lease a building or protect intellectual property. They may have a tax dispute or want to buy a competitor. They might want to hire a scientist from overseas and they need immigration help. These corporations didn't want to have to pay for seven different lawyers to accomplish these legal tasks, like the billion dollar companies do. It didn't make financial sense for them to have seven different lawyers to call. They wanted one firm, one phone number, and one trusted legal counsel who understood the nuances of their businesses and who's done all or most of those things for others in their industry. We needed to understand the potential impact on the business and intuitively know the urgency and priority of these issues and the corresponding legal tasks.

Here's an example. Clinical laboratories receive specimens via FedEx air and ground all over the country. If a package of specimens happens to break on the plane and leaks all over the cargo, they'll get a phone call from the Federal Aviation Administration (FAA) telling them they're going to be fined $1000 a day until they prove their packaging is up to FAA regulations. A mid-size laboratory firm won't want to have to pay an FAA lawyer to help them with their problem. They want to call up the lawyer who specializes in laboratories and ask, "Hey, has this every happened to any one of your laboratory clients?" Because we were those lawyers, we could confidently answer, "As a matter of fact, yes. Let me pull up my FAA cheat sheet for laboratory specimen transport and tell you what you need to do. I'll call the FAA and figure out how to solve this and get back to you soon." And thus we continued to grow the clients' trust in our abilities.

Now, we are not experts in FAA regulations, but we have taken the time to fully research this very issue. We have competence in administrative law. We understand how to review statutes, rules, regulations, and opinions from an administrative agency. We know how to nail down the relevant and applicable legal authorities. We know how to research other articles or instances for which this issue has become important. We have the confidence to engage the FAA officials to understand their interests and the parameters within which they are actually operating, sometimes, irrespective of what the actual rules say on paper. We can chart a course to resolution in the most advantageous manner possible for our client. (Spoiler alert: in most cases it is an explanatory letter from the firm's client.)

We have found that effective communication is often the key to resolution of most of these types of matters. If you're the laboratory with this problem, good luck finding (and paying) an FAA lawyer who understands this particular issue for laboratories and the full impact it has on laboratory operations as well as we do. You'd be better off calling the general counsel of UPS or better yet, one of your competitors. With a savvy attorney like us who specializes in your business niche, you're taken care of.

At the same time, just because the firm is offering a good variety of legal skills doesn't mean we had to know or do everything ourselves. Sometimes being a specialist means knowing when to associate with another lawyer. We found ourselves in that position primarily when dealing with criminal matters like ongoing investigations or tax matters involving audits. This association need not be complicated, either. We might need to simply make a phone call to supplement our information or to get a quick case review and opinion. We could also opt to give the matter to another attorney while we work side by side with them for our client. There are many ways to collaborate or benefit from our association with other lawyers and get the work done at the level of excellence we aim for. However, as we will discuss, it is important for a firm to assess where to set healthy boundaries within these associations.

In this chapter we've fleshed out the cornerstone of our small law success strategy – business niche specialization. We've identified the five key characteristics of business niches that we believe have made for the optimal choice of business niche that enabled us to found and operate our successful, independent law practice.

In the next chapter, we turn to the tactics we have utilized that enabled us to successfully execute the business niche specialization strategy. While several of the tactics are applicable to all lawyers and firms, the specific set of tactics discussed in this book are uniquely suited to a law firm with a business niche specialization. They are drawn from our own experience and they worked for us largely because they matched our business niche specialization strategy. We predict they will work for you as you adopt and execute your own particular business niche specialization strategy. We'll discuss efficient business development for your niche-centric law practice. We examine what is essentially a business development playbook that will help you grow your business quickly, methodically and effectively. From investing in educating yourself about your niche, to developing relationships, to using smart marketing tactics, you won't have to wait long to find your law firm thriving.

# 4. Small law business development

Now that you have an understanding of how to select a lucrative business niche for your small firm, you have within your grasp the first and most important step to achieving astonishing success in your independent law firm. Your particular business niche specialization will be the foundational strategy that allows your firm to grow and be profitable in such a short period of time that your BigLaw colleagues will be dumbfounded. You have what it takes to set yourself apart, draw in and maintain clients large and small, distinguish yourself as an expert, and earn exceptional revenues.

But with business niche specialization defining your business model, you'll still need to learn the tactics that will allow you to leverage this strategy into a successful, sustainable business. This chapter, and those that follow, provide the tactics that will allow you to fully execute your business niche business model. The first set of tactics pertains to business development – helping you swiftly build your practice in the initial stages of your firm's growth. We'll share with you what we did to effectively grow our practice and we'll guide you to build your own client base and acquire the clients and matters that will propel you to success as quickly as possible. The experiences and lessons described in this chapter will serve as your business development playbook. By adopting these tactics, you can quickly get working on matters within a chosen business niche, gain relevant and marketable experience, grow profitably, and ensure the growth and long-term success of your independent law firm.

Most new businesses expect that the way to build their revenues is to invest capital in typical outreach efforts: marketing, advertising, website presence, social media, and the like. But our experience has shown us a much more effective path for niche-centric law firms who are eager to grow quickly and consistently.

We took three critical and fundamental steps on our path to success, steps that we now recommend to anyone following the business niche specialization strategy. First, we educated ourselves about our niche, clinical laboratories, extremely well. We went from complete beginners to respected experts – from 0 to 60 – in the legal issues that would impact our prospective clients within our niche. Second, we focused on building relationships and establishing contacts. We concentrated on developing a network of clients and prospective clients, as well as the players with whom they interacted and relied on for the operation and development of their businesses. These were the vendors, suppliers, and consulting companies who understood our value and who might refer business to us. This was a process of building our Rolodex and learning who the potential clients were that we would want to represent.

In this chapter, we'll present some obvious and some not-so-obvious marketing tactics that will make it easier for your target market to find you and hire you.

## BECOME THE EXPERT

To run a successful law firm within a particular business niche, it is essential to become one of the most highly knowledgeable lawyers in that particular business niche and command a depth of understanding of your industry for which the decision makers will want to hire you. But, as we learned, educating yourself can be a challenge for a variety of reasons. There are probably no courses taught in law schools about the issues that concern particular industries or business niches. This was certainly true for us; many law schools did not teach a course on healthcare law, let alone laws relating to the development, operation, and regulation of clinical laboratories. There probably aren't any Continuing Legal Education classes (CLEs) to cover those areas and there are likely only very few lawyers doing it, either. Such was the case for our firm and clinical laboratories. (However, that void will work in your favor in the long run.)

But there are a number of things that you can do to go from knowing nothing to becoming a relative expert in your field pretty quickly. We'll share with you the things that we did as we started out in our niche to swiftly inform and educate ourselves for our prospective clients.

For one, we learned as much as we could from other attorneys who had gone before us, attorneys who had done their own research in our niche and were aware of the legal issues that prospective clients within that niche have to face. Luckily, Yussuf was able to zero in on some of the very few attorneys operating within the clinical laboratory space because they were representing clients of his consulting firm. We Googled them to find out who they were and what they were doing. We analyzed whatever work they did that applied to our business niche. We read the articles they published and followed them on social media. Heck, when we could, we read the books and articles in which they were published. We attended CLEs that offered them. We did whatever was necessary to download whatever they knew that we didn't know that was pertinent to our niche.

Sometimes attorneys actually enjoy taking time out of their schedules (gasp) to mentor younger lawyers. If you feel comfortable with that, you can approach one of them from the perspective of a mentee and ask to pick their brains. They may even be willing to share some model documents or opinions, discuss how they approach issues, or talk about which resources are helpful in your niche practice. It typically does not hurt to ask, but be mindful that you may very soon be competing with this lawyer for clients, and at some point, he may choose to disclose that not so long ago you were seeking his advice. Certainly, if you are still in a BigLaw job or at a firm, then this could be an opportunity, depending on how skilled you are at wrangling some free minutes from a partner or senior associate.

We recommend that you do what we did: read as many books about your chosen niche as you can find. Find books online or in bookstores, books within your field or that cover the legal issues that are pertinent to your particular business niche. When we started out in laboratory law, we found an excellent set of books covering antifraud and abuse rules, regulations, and laws and these gave us a tremendous starting point to grow our insights into the issues with which we would be grappling in our practice. Reading and researching gave us a very valuable understanding of the context surrounding the regulations that affect our particular niche. Then, we took it upon ourselves to find and read the opinions that were written on them and the real-life cases that dealt with those regulations. We dug deeper to find real-world examples and specifics that helped us get a comprehensive grasp of the complexity within our field. We were building our own knowledge base and we didn't underestimate its value to our success.

Read, read, read. Read the news. Read industry blogs if you can. We found a legal blog, *The Pathology Blawg* (yes, really), that pathologists use to stay informed about what's happening in the industry outside of their own laboratories. It was a perfect reference for us. Almost every article had a nugget that helped us get where we needed to be to represent clients within our niche. It also became a go-to outlet for us to publish articles – another business development tactic that we'll cover later in this chapter. The articles offered a great excuse to call up a client or prospective client and say, "Did you see the article about X? These are my thoughts on how it does or does not apply to your business … ."

As you collect information, it's wise to be practical and organize your library of resources and references. There will be a time in your future, when you'll need to chase down specific issues, and you just might already have some of it within your grasp. You'll want to be able to find that opinion letter that you read two years ago, now that the issue has emerged as significant with one of your clients. As your research deepens, you'll also inevitably scare up more material to supplement your gaps of knowledge in the field, and you'll have a convenient place to file them all.

If you really want a crash course in your niche of choice, you can place yourself right in the center of things by working with a consulting company, which is how Yussuf discovered the laboratory niche. Especially if you've picked a niche that's new to you and you don't know what you're doing yet, it might be a good idea to first take a job with a consulting company or at least do some contract work with one. The benefit of this is that you get to see the full range of issues of your prospective clients and you're forced to think through them from their business perspective. You learn what's important to the businesses and the clients within your niche. And you learn exactly what they're looking for in law firms and how you can eventually add value to their business when you do go off on your own.

Yussuf had no idea that he was going to eventually launch his own firm when he took a job as inside counsel for a consulting company that provided turnkey development and operations solutions for laboratories. They worked on concerns of laboratory development, laboratory billing, and other issues related to the operations of laboratories. Clients were existing laboratories, medical providers seeking to build laboratory capabilities, and groups and individuals seeking to develop brand new laboratory facilities. The experience gave Yussuf tremendous exposure to the legal issues pertaining to developing and operating these laboratories. The company regularly scheduled meetings with prospective clients who were interviewing consulting companies for help building new laboratories. Somewhat surprisingly, 75% of the questions that the potential clients brought up were legal questions: *Can we do this? How do we do this legally? How do we set ourselves up to comply with these laws?*

The education Yussuf received was priceless. But he didn't need to spend years and years chained to his desk, working 90+ hours per week, turning comments for partners to get such an education. He stayed at the consulting firm for about six months and then it was time for him to open a firm of his own. At that point, he probably knew as much about the wide array of legal issues that prospective clients would want help with as nearly 95% of all lawyers. Let that sink in. He knew as much, if not more, on the legal topics within this specific niche, than 95% of all lawyers out there. When he participated in the numerous conference calls that were set up with senior healthcare attorneys and partners at prestigious BigLaw firms, Yussuf consistently understood the legal issues more completely, and was able to solve their problems more effectively, than the attending senior partner. This is the level of expertise you will need in order to successfully implement your business niche specialization strategy and grow your independent firm.

We also want to point out the value of presenting yourself as a problem-solver, not just an issue-spotter. Traditionally, BigLaw's tendency is to focus on identifying as many issues as possible and briefing and researching them exhaustively. They're not necessarily searching for the most creative and efficient ways to solve the business' problems, at least until they've received their billable target for that client. It was during the conference calls that Yussuf learned that problem-solving skills were a key asset to earning new clients' trust and business. In short, being an expert in your business niche will get you clients, but being a problem-solver is how you keep them.

Keep in mind that the business niche specialization business strategy will also require a breadth of expertise – not just a depth of it – for you to accelerate your success as an independent small firm. We've talked about the importance of providing a diversity of legal skills earlier; business niche specialization will only work if you can sell your firm as one that can handle any legal issue that comes up for a client, with very, very few exceptions. We learned quickly to be as close to a full-service shop as possible; we set up our firm to be fully capable of providing virtually every service that our clients would inevitably need: transactional skills, litigation, employee agreements, labor law, bankruptcy, intellectual property, mergers and acquisitions, and even some criminal issues.

Just to clarify, we never felt that we had to master every skill ourselves. For example, we never touched a tax matter for any client, laboratory or otherwise. We recommend that you set your firm up to have the skill base to do things well. For example, if you're not a litigator, recognize that you're going to need to do some litigation in your firm sooner or later. To accomplish that, you could partner with another lawyer who does litigation. Or participate in CLEs. Or you might bring on a contractor to help you with the litigation. Whatever creative solution you can come up with: do it. You have to be able to handle the full breadth of legal issues that arise for your clients.

## CONTACTS, CONTACTS, CONTACTS

A Florida-based lawyer we knew was approached by a neurologist solo practitioner from rural Georgia for help with a small insurance dispute. The lawyer referred him to us here in Atlanta. The neurologist didn't have a huge legal budget or vast legal needs, but we helped him out with a small corporate task and made it affordable to him. A little later, he told the laboratory that he sent his work to about us, and that laboratory eventually reached out to us and became a client. They are now one of our largest clients and we have them on a full retainer basis.

Almost every business is based on building relationships and the legal profession is no exception. It's simple addition: the more contacts you make, the more people you'll know who respect you and can refer you. Along with your genuine interest in their welfare, your efforts to connect to the people at all levels of your industry niche will pay you back in huge returns. Whether they are vendors, suppliers, consulting companies, or other attorneys in your industry, it will be worth the time and effort to form and sustain good relationships with them. A large portion of your business growth and development will depend on referrals from the people you know *and the people they know*. Don't underestimate how much of an impact your relationships make on building your business.

We've suggested earlier that you could work with a consulting company to inform yourself about the many potential issues of prospective clients in your business niche. But there's a second valuable benefit to being part of a consulting agency: you'll be exposed to a great number of contacts and clients in the industry with whom you can establish connections. You might just want to represent them later as an independent lawyer. At a consulting company, you can also get the inside scoop on who the decision makers are in the field and figure out who are the phonies and who are the legitimate clients. Be sure to consider all roles – even non-legal titles – as you will still likely be exposed to legal issues facing these clients. Consulting companies can be an incredible resource for contacts for your future.

You can find people to connect with in the oddest of places. For example, there's nothing improper about getting to know the people on the other side of the transaction table when all is said and done. You can follow up with them after the work on that particular matter is complete. Of course, you should be careful to avoid potential conflicts of interest. But you can easily call and ask about their needs going forward. Were they impressed with your services? Is there anything further they'd like to know about you? They'll remember you for it.

Jacob's mentor, one of the most successful commercial real-estate lawyers in New York, frequently found that doing an exceptional job when potential clients are sitting across the negotiating table was a great way to pitch for business. Great lawyers often succeed in demonstrating their value to non-clients and turning them into clients. This is the mindset you must have whenever you enter into a negotiation or dispute; think of the adversary as another potential client. Always conduct yourself with ethics and class and demonstrate superior value to those across the table. They'll conclude that not only are you a better expert in their business niche, but you are also probably cheaper than the prestigious BigLaw (non-niche) lawyer that they hired.

And there's nothing wrong with schmoozing in the old-fashioned sense. Go to industry conventions and trade shows; they're great for meeting all sorts of folks in your industry. Just be sure to go to the ones where the decision makers for your potential clients are. Don't go to a convention of lawyers who are trying to do the same thing you're doing. We wouldn't go to healthcare lawyers' convention to meet clients, for example. We may hope that several GC's go, but our experience tells us not to expect it. Even if they do show up, they are inundated with other suitor law firms and they are not altogether focused on building more relationships at these events. We go to laboratory technology conventions because our potential clients – owners and operators of the laboratories – will be there. Inevitably, they have legal issues they need help with, and they want to draw from outside influences and improve their business, so we have their ear. It is an outstanding venue to impress upon them that we are experienced experts and knowledgeable leaders in our industry.

While we were expanding our network of connections, we made a point not to abandon our existing client base. Of course we were always on the lookout for new clients, but we also worked to feed and nurture our relationships with our existing clients. Even now, we continue to schedule occasional check-in calls to find out how they are. It delivers a powerful message that we care about them and that we don't only call them when there's a billable matter to discuss. It's a free call, after all. We ask them open-ended questions: *What's on your mind? What issues and challenges are you facing? What's keeping you up at night? Maybe there's something we can do about it? How can we help improve your business?* Our check-in calls can sometimes yield new work or foster a relationship with a new person that leads to new work. When we do this, we often, but not always, get a call back that leads to more billable work.

Sometimes when a client is facing a business/operations issue, their initial call might not be to their lawyer. But by being in touch with them, your experience as a business niche expert might mean that you can relay experiences of other similar businesses who have faced similar situations. In this way, you can help solve their problems, even if it is not a "traditional" legal matter.

The more people you know, the better. However, when you know a lot of actors within an industry, you can sometimes run into sticky situations. Inevitably some of these folks will not get along or will fall out of favor with each other. These mutual relations sour and such developments can be tricky for the law firm to handle, as your natural inclination is to remain somewhat neutral.

For example, since we launched our firm, we have formed relationships with quite a few billing companies. And since nearly all mid-sized laboratories hire outside billing companies to handle the complexities of laboratory and medical billing, quite a number of them have referred prospective clients to us. But we had one laboratory client that ended up suing a billing company with whom we had a friendly relationship. Now, upon a thoughtful analysis, there was nothing that legally prevented us from representing our client and suing the billing company, but because we were on good terms with them, we knew we had a difficult decision to make. We realized that if we were going to go ahead and sue them, it'd be unlikely that they would refer any new clients to us ever again. We'd lose that very beneficial referral channel. But we also knew that if we thought the billing company was in the wrong, we had a responsibility to proceed for our client. Further, it would simply be a bad reflection on us to remain associated with them – if they were unethical or incompetent, we wouldn't want to be associated with them anyhow. So we chose to proceed with the lawsuit. Sometimes you need to sever relationships even with those that have been good to you in the past if the situation warrants it. For the short term, we expected that the kind words about our firm would dry up and we hoped that no unkind words were said. But for the long term, we felt it was the right decision.

Things can sometimes get uncomfortable or even sensitive when you're representing different actors within the same industry that are somewhat averse to each other, but you have to learn to be comfortable with it and deal with it as best you can. After all, somebody you're working with today might end up on the other side of the table tomorrow. You may have a client who has sworn vengeance against a vendor, supplier, or even client that you work with owing to some business issue. While it may be an uncomfortable situation, it is where ethics come into play. And it may also benefit you in the long run as you get known as someone in the industry who does the honorable thing, especially if you become known as the lawyer that deals with highest-quality suppliers, vendors, and ancillary service providers. Again, this underscores the importance of conducting yourself with ethics and class.

Dinners have long been a staple for consummating deals and developing business relationships in the legal industry, and for good reason. They can be very valuable to you. Besides the conversation you have at the table, dinner connections have a habit of branching out into more contacts and opportunities and often lead to surprising and very lucrative outcomes. You can never predict how the chain of connections will branch out and lead to someone who knows someone who knows someone. So when you're stressed out at the end of a stressful week, facing the prospect of having to meet and talk to a contact that you feel you want to raincheck, see it through. It might just end up leading you to a huge client. You just never know.

Here's a rule by which we operate: no matter who invites whom to dinner, we don't ever let a client pay for dinner. It's on us. Period. If we do find ourselves in the position of thinking the client should be the one to pay, we see it as a signal to re-evaluate them as a client and review why we considered having dinner with them in the first place. We figure that if we're not getting enough value from them, then we should move on. And we also give ourselves permission to turn down a dinner invitation whenever necessary.

It goes without saying, but is still worth mentioning, that you should keep your client contact information well organized for easy retrieval. It's your way of keeping your eye on the future. If you find yourself dealing with an issue in Colorado, you're going to want to be able to go back to your records of the Colorado company you worked with at the consulting company and see what you did back then. Save your notes and your emails for all of the cases you're working on. And if you're at a consulting company, expecting to eventually go off on your own, keep a record of the issues you deal with there, too. You're well within your rights to jot down notes of what you're learning and doing and keep them for your personal reference.

Finally, when you're just starting out as a small law firm specializing in a particular business niche, you want to be saying "yes" a lot. Accept virtually every offer that comes your way. In fact, you should only reject work under very limited circumstances – if they're asking you to do something illegal or something that violates conflict of interest rules. We refer back to the story of our physician friend. You'd think that a solo practice neurosurgeon in a small (and we mean *small*) rural town in southern Georgia, with no plans for expansion, would not typically incur *any* legal issues in a given year, much less expensive ones. So you'd probably be inclined to think that it wouldn't be worth taking one on as a client. But we did, and we charged him a reasonable price for our legal services. As a result of our good work, he recommended us to a laboratory that had high-value legal matters and that turned into a big client for our firm. The lesson? Take on all legal work early on, including seemingly "small" matters. They just might lead to more lucrative work.

## "TRADITIONAL" MARKETING TACTICS

After you've immersed yourself in the legal issues and concerns of the companies in your business niche and have become a relative expert on these topics, and while you're building relationships with current and potential clients, there are now several powerful (albeit more "traditional") marketing tactics you should implement to expand your contact network and begin to land increasingly lucrative and loyal business in fairly short order.

First, the basics. You obviously want to brand yourself and have at least a minimal digital online presence to reinforce your status as industry expert. Have a website that announces that you specialize in representing providers within your business niche. But don't go crazy with this. You don't need, and shouldn't bother trying to build, a tremendous web presence that drives thousands of people to your website every day. Your web presence is there to reinforce your niche and respond to specific targeted searches pertaining to your niche only. Don't bother plunking down 100, 50, or even 20 grand to generate a huge, elaborate website. Something simple is all you need to reinforce who you are. Our website has always been a simple static WordPress site that includes biographies, representative matters, and contact information.

As with other professional fields, publishing articles will go a long way to promote your firm, your expertise, and your brand. This shouldn't be difficult because there are tons of developing legal issues and there aren't a lot of people addressing them in publications. A good goal to have would be to write an article on some new legal issue or highlight a case within your business niche every month. Or explain how an existing area of law affects your particular business niche.

For example, we wrote an article about how trade secrets apply to laboratories. We're not intellectual property experts but we are very familiar with a number of specific issues about intellectual property and trade secrets and how they apply to the laboratories we represent. What steps do they need to take? What do they need to watch out for? What trade secrets issues come up for laboratories? These are the kinds of questions we asked and answered. Focus on writing articles that explain to your current and prospective clients how to solve a problem. Reinforce your expertise as well as your track record of helping clients solve problems in creative ways. When they're published, send the articles to existing clients or prospective clients you want to establish a relationship with. You'll definitely make an impression.

Writing blogs is another way to establish yourself as a thought leader in your niche. You probably are not familiar with the *Pathology Blawg*. (It no longer exists.) Probably every CEO of every single laboratory in the country read it daily and their general counsels probably read it weekly, if not daily. We became best friends with the individual who wrote the blog and soon started writing articles for the blog ourselves. It gave us tremendous exposure and set us up as industry experts precisely within our target niche. Once we published content in the *Pathology Blawg*, laboratories began calling us with questions. The answers we gave would turn into more detailed conversations, and those conversations soon turned into requests for our legal services. Of course, it won't happen that way for you every time. But this is an incredibly cheap and easy way to corral the focused attention of the most valuable players in your niche.

You can also start your own blog. This will require a bit more social media presence, marketing, and engagement on your part. We are not experts on this topic but there are many resources available to drive engagement with a blog of your own. Keep in mind, however, that you want your blog in front of the decision makers of your potential clients. Writing a blog that they don't read is not going to yield you any benefits.

Our presence in industry publications went a long way to reinforce our authority on the topic of our niche. During cases, for example, when we were introduced to the other side's CEO, we mentioned that we had been writing in such and such publication and asked, *Oh, by the way, have you seen any of our articles?* No matter who you are, it's important to demonstrate that you have expertise. But it is especially important to small law firms.

Where do you find ideas to write about? As a specialist in your business niche, you'll have your ear to the ground and you'll easily hear about the juicy issues that the people in your industry care about. If you notice you keep getting calls about the same questions and issues from your clients, it's time to write an article. Write about actual legal problems you have solved. Any matter you handle for a client has the potential to be the subject of an article or case study for client advisory emails or newsletters. There will be plenty of other people who have those same questions. After only a couple of months, you'll have plenty of topics for your articles.

When it comes to writing articles, we believe that the beauty of it is that almost anybody can do it. We have interns who write first drafts of articles for us. While the initial drafting can be time-consuming, and you're not billing anybody for it, it's a very effective method to draw in the clients you seek.

Vendors, suppliers, and consulting companies can be great resources for news about your industry. We would often glean valuable news from billing companies or clients and then we'd write a Client Advisory alerting them that we were just told about an emerging legal issue facing a lot of businesses in their industry. Of course, any article you write must be blasted to your Rolodex as a client advisory. Let them know that you wanted to put it on their radar and explain it to them. Show them that you are on top of it and can address any legal issues that come up for them. This tactic has been tremendously effective in building our industry authority and credibility.

We learned that clients love it when their lawyer is out there with their finger on the pulse of the industry. They want to know that you represent a lot of other companies like theirs and that you know – and have gotten a stamp of approval from – some of the big players in the industry. It's a big selling point too that will help you win over new clients. Use that to your advantage. Further, clients love hearing that you're dealing with their particular issue with another company in the industry. As long as you keep the details confidential, you can let them know that you're involved with the matter elsewhere.

Writing for industry publications is effective, targeted marketing. It will be much more successful for you than slapping a billboard on the highway.

Which brings up the brief topic of what you should *not* do. It should go without saying, but you *don't* need to paste your firm's name and smiling faces on billboards, TV commercials, or in national magazine ads. Business niches are typically not geographically specific. You're not a New York divorce lawyer or a Texas water rights expert. Even if you are a Texas water rights expert, you are probably going to rely more on internet technology than billboards to find the decision makers who will want to hire you for such work. You might possibly find a worthy trade publication to advertise in, if there is one, but it may not be cost-effective. The best marketing you can do is to follow the tactics we mentioned above: press the flesh, nurture word of mouth, connect with a consultant or vendor. The type of client you want is not one that will see a billboard and call an attorney. So don't waste your time or money.

## EASY STUFF FOR FREE

Whenever you reach out to potential clients, it's highly likely that they already have a lawyer or that they've worked with lawyers in the past. So when you're building your business, it's smart to find ways to still be the most appealing offer in the room. And there's nothing more appealing than doing something valuable for free. As a new, small, independent firm with a business niche specialty, we found that one of the keys to winning over new clients was to offer to do simple, easy tasks for free. By doing so, we could show off that we were more nimble, more friendly, more available, and yes, more affordable than the other guys.

As one of only a few experts in your niche, you are in a great position to do this. For example, an investment group might want to set up a new laboratory business and so they're looking to generate business formation documents to help them do that. They don't really need you for that and they certainly don't need to pay anyone a lot of money for it. It's inexpensive and they may be quite able to do it for themselves. But if you offer to help them in their early stages of business development, you'll make big inroads in winning their trust. By working with you, they'll see your quality of work, sample your expertise in the issues that concern them, and many of them will come back for more from you. These simple openings can easily lead to a longer-term relationship over more complex legal matters that will make a huge impact on their organization. We've used this tactic with many potential clients who have crossed paths with us and ended up forging lucrative long-term attorney–client relationships.

There will be an endless supply of companies who have questions about particular, discrete issues that won't necessarily require a lot of time or effort for you to solve for them. Maybe it's just a quirky research assignment. Can they bill this code for this procedure under these circumstances? It may only take half a day for you to call up your contact at one of your billing companies, read through the billing manual, and come up with a solid answer that they can use within their business operations. So go ahead and do that for them. No charge.

Then call them up and fill them in. "Just as a courtesy, I went ahead and followed up on the research question you asked me about. Here's the research I came up with and it's relatively simple. Let me tell you what I found out … ." Or, if the conclusions aren't so simple, let them know that, too. "Hi Andrew, I wanted to let you know that I researched the issue you asked me about and it looks like it's a lot more complicated than we thought. I don't know how important this is to your organization, but in order to get the answer, this is what we'd need to look at and verify." Your initial research was free. Now they're in a position to pay you for just a little work to get some valuable questions answered. And with that, your foot is in the door.

Here's the upshot: get yourself in front of people. Demonstrate your ability to answer their questions and provide valuable information. Become a resource for more. Establish that you are a problem-solver, not just a problem-identifier.

Here's how this tactic will help you stand out. When they hear about a legal issue, most lawyers want to immediately dive into a 20-hour, 10-page research memo. But the decision makers within the types of business niches that fit our criteria for small law firms often just want a two-sentence email. And they want it in an hour. They don't have time to read a 10-page memo. They want to use the answers they seek to make a decision about some changes to their operations right away. So keep it simple and give them what they want: short answers in a short period of time. And when you do that, you demonstrate that you care about their business, that you value their relationship, and that little research efforts like this one won't make or break your firm. You're letting them know that you have plenty of big things going on, and you don't have to scrape for little bits of work.

Having said all this, it's important to remember that you can't let your firm get bogged down in free assignments. You have to know where to set your limits, when there's more to do than your business will allow you to do for free. You need to be prepared to have the conversation to tell your clients that you need to start charging for your next set of services. If you've done it correctly, the client will recognize that they need what they're asking for to run their business, and they won't balk at the change in status. And because you've set the precedent with the free work you've done, they'll know that you've got their interests in mind and you have a business to run, after all, and you're not just taking advantage of them.

As counter-intuitive as it may seem, another highly valuable tactic we've used is cold-calling and cold-emailing. We've pulled some of our biggest clients out of nowhere by emailing them when we found out that they had a big case going on. It's pretty simple to do. Scan the news and the court dockets for disputes, cases and investigations that involve any of the people or companies that you'd like to represent. Then reach out to them directly. "I read that you're involved in XYZ lawsuit and I wanted to let you know that I've handled similar lawsuits." Or, "Hey, I see you're being investigated for ABC. I've handled similar investigations and I'd like to help you out." Or, "I see you're contemplating this type of purchase or transaction. I have experience doing so with another laboratory and it worked out very well for us. Please give me a call."

This worked for us in a big way. A Texas laboratory was getting sued by one of the big health insurance companies. We saw a small write-up about the lawsuit in an obscure laboratory/healthcare publication. We cold-called their general counsel and told them we'd like to offer our laboratory expertise and prior experience negotiating the same issue with the same insurance company. They already had a lawyer but they wanted us on their team. Their lawyer was a big name. But as our work progressed, it became clear that we had a better grasp of the industry and the overall picture of how the adversaries were handling these types of disputes and negotiations. We built more trust with the client. It turns out that their first lawyer was great at fighting but not as deft at negotiating and reconciling. The client ended up being a long-term client of ours. When they became involved in another, similar suit, we were the first call they made.

## MINNOWS AND WHALES

If you noticed, we've been focusing our discussion on engaging the relatively smaller companies with more predictable legal needs at first, since they help pay the bills, they enrich your knowledge of your niche, and they're potentially referral sources for more business. But let's be honest, you're not going to build a million-dollar practice by trolling for minnows. You do need to eventually earmark a good portion of your client development efforts for landing the big whales of the industry.

What we call "whale" clients are typically midsize companies that have been in the industry for at least a year or two and that have significant monthly revenue. To a small firm specializing in a business niche, a whale client is a company that is capable of spending at least a million dollars a year on legal services if their business depends on it. They're the ones that will probably have legal issues that they'll need your help with in the future, although they might not currently have any live ones on the table. Whales can also be mid-sized clients who find themselves in a whale-sized legal predicament. The predicament might be regulatory or litigious in nature but it can just as well be a new transaction. We've had clients that engaged us to represent them as they purchased several rural hospitals all over the country. As you get more exposure to the whales in your niche, you need to be patient and carefully assess the likelihood that they'll eventually need your expert legal services.

Now, most lawyers assume that they should only go after these large, rich companies and try to land them as clients. After all, they figure, if you're going to go fishing, you might as well seek out the big fish. They can provide food for a lot of meals, right? But the problem is that whales are few and far between. In the meantime, you still have to pay the utility bills and the payroll. That's where the "minnows" come in: those smaller businesses who bring in smaller matters, but together make up the meat and potatoes of your business – especially when you're just getting started. They like your work, they have their own business connections, and with their help you grow your referral network. You might go to dinner with them, bump into someone else they know, and they introduce you as their lawyer. And your business grows. Filling your roster with small business matters will assist you in accomplishing two very important tasks: generating revenue and connecting to your community. Both will sustain you, even as a new firm.

In the early days as an independent law firm, you won't have a clear idea of who the whales in your business niche are and you probably won't have access to them just yet. So while you're bringing in as much minnow business as possible, it's important that you also keep your eyes open for the whales. As you begin to land them, you need to then make it a priority to acquire more of them.

When we were getting started, we signed every laboratory we could. Some had not begun operations yet. Some were making millions of dollars per month. Some were physician-owned laboratories – single physician practices that had installed their own laboratory capabilities to test their own patients. The latter tended not to generate complex matters that involved lots of legal work. So while we cast our net with as big a reach as we could, we focused on finding the laboratories that were making millions of dollars per month.

At the same time, you should be on the lookout for legal matters that are going to generate value for your company. Helping a client hire an employee is not going to move the revenue needle for you. Negotiating a CEO agreement is not going to do much for you financially, either. But lawsuits from a competitor or a private insurance company or audits from a private insurance company will. The same goes for a mergers and acquisitions transaction where your client wants to buy a competitor or buy a line of their business.

Part of what it takes to sign large clients is to know your niche and to know how much business is out there for the potential clients and their potential assignments within that niche. It's why we describe the secret sauce of an optimal business niche as having the characteristics we described in the last chapter. If you picked a business niche with a lot of startups and nobody's generating any revenue, it's not going to be a lucrative niche for you. If you've picked a niche that's completely stagnant, with no growth and no big lawsuits, then there's not likely to be a lot of big assignments out there for you. You will not find enough whales in this niche to grow a prosperous legal practice, to the tune of million dollar annual billings. But a niche that is emerging, profitable, mid-sized, and has some complexity to it will have a good catch of whales needing your expertise.

Of course, you still have to be patient. Just because you landed a big client, it doesn't mean that they're going to generate a whale of an assignment for you. Still, you can't cherry-pick and show favoritism, either. When you get a large, complex assignment, you can't just disregard the other big clients you work with that don't have a lot going on at the moment. Inevitably they're going to have a big issue arise and you want to be the first call that they make when that happens. Which is why we suggest that you constantly and consistently nurture your relationships with your existing client base, no matter how active or inactive. Don't lose touch or neglect them. Stay in the mix.

As your business develops and you gain more clients, large and small, you should make a habit of taking a bird's eye view of your practice to see who are the whales and what are the whale assignments you have at the current time. If you haven't had them for a while, you need to go back to the basics of your business development playbook. You need to get back out in the public eye.

You need to go to trade shows, publish some articles. Of course, as a small firm, you can get quite busy and sometimes the instinct is to cut back on client development activities when there's a lot of work going on. But if you do, you might be hurting business six months from now, when the assignment that's keeping you so busy now starts winding down. Business development is an ongoing, never-ending effort that stokes the fires of your emerging practice.

There were times when we decided we needed to trim the minnows. The Pareto principle holds that 20% of your clients will give you 80% of your headaches. If that 20% is made up of minnows, you need to get rid of some of them if you find it impossible to reduce their burden on your resources. While it's preferable to cut down on the time spent on phone calls and emails for a non-productive client, sometimes more dramatic action is necessary. After all, the cost of spending time on a burdensome minnow is the time you aren't available to spend cultivating the next whale of a client. This culling decision is not always about money. It might be the risk, stress, or extra effort that has you decide that a paying client is not worth your firm's time. On the other hand, minnows often lead to whales. If you're building is goodwill from maintaining the relationship, it might make sense to keep the client in spite of the short-term cost. Again, like a lot of things about running your firm, it is a balancing act. You need to keep on top of it to make sure your relationships still make sense for everybody.

In this chapter, we discussed the key tactics to start growing a small law firm, specializing in a lucrative business niche, quickly and effectively. First, setting the groundwork by becoming an expert in your niche – and doing what you need to do to be recognized as such – begins to set you apart. Second, building relationships and connecting to people at all levels of your industry niche will help stoke your marketing and referral machinery. Finally, using wise marketing tactics helps you maximize opportunities and minimize time and money spent on those things that bring no returns.

In the next chapter, we'll reveal several billing practices that we've found to be extremely valuable and essential to a small law firm startup. We'll introduce you to flexible billing strategies that fit your size and that will make you more attractive to your potential clients. And we'll discuss essentials to planning and to communication within your organization that will help you avoid pitfalls and make the most of your company resources.

# 5.  Small law; smart billing

Being a small firm means that your financial relationships with your clients are different from what you'd experience at BigLaw. As a small firm, you have an opportunity to establish deeper rapport and greater transparency to support the essential foundations for long-term trust. You must listen to and understand your clients' business so that you can serve them most effectively. From a financial perspective, a smaller profile offers the unique ability to adopt more attractive billing arrangements for clients while still making a profit for the law firm. Holding hard and fast to rigid rules that apply to any and all clients might work for large law firms, but it is not advantageous and is too confining for your small firm. At the same time, a dogged willingness to be flexible without any planning or constant communication can sink a small, independent law firm just as fast as billing rigidity.

We have three guiding principles that we adopted for our firm through real-life trial and error, and which we recommend small firms use to approach billing: flexibility, planning, and communication. With these guiding principles in place, we predict that you are highly likely to achieve sustainable and mutually beneficial financial arrangements with your clients.

## FLEXIBLE BILLING

When it comes to billing practices for a business niche law firm, we have learned that flexibility is a key value-add for clients. We've been successful at building trust with clients in large part owing to the choices we provide in our billing policies. We consider flat per transaction fees, monthly fee schedules, hourly billing, and retainers—or a combination of all of these—when we talk to prospective clients or discuss the fee arrangement for a new matter. And we can do so because we are less constrained by a large body of partners and/or high overhead costs. We look for a solution that is most amenable to the success of our firm and to the interests of our client. Whenever possible, we create an arrangement that the client has helped craft. That way, the client has a higher degree of psychological commitment to the billing arrangement than if we were to solely dictate the terms of our engagement.

As a small firm, you don't have the overhead that you find at large firms: overhead that requires massive revenues to bankroll. You have a wider spectrum of choices, you don't have to please anyone else, and you can negotiate arrangements that are most fitting to your business and to your clients.

Take the time to arrive at the best billing arrangements by evaluating all of your billing inputs. What do we mean when we say "billing inputs"? These are the firm-based, internal factors and the client-based, external factors that will contribute to your ability to determine the proper billing method to use for each individual client or matter. Both are equally important.

Internal factors are the easiest billing inputs to determine since you have access to most, if not all, of the critical information about your own firm. If you find you are lacking information about your firm, take the time to seek it out or cull it from existing data, organize it, and filter it to obtain the relevant information you need. This is where practice management software or tools can really be of help. We don't discuss these tools in much depth in this book because there are plenty of books, articles, reviews, and product comments that can help you evaluate them.

For example, you'll want to consider the type of legal matter you're pursuing and your firm's expertise to handle such a matter relative to that of other lawyers and firms in the market for such business. You'll factor in your firm's overall position in the legal industry and your target business niche, your ability to charge higher rates—both in practice and hypothetically—and even whether you want to put lower-cost arrangements in place with this client to reel in anticipated future business.

You'll also want to evaluate the costs associated with the action and assess whether those costs are traditionally borne by the firm or the client. What's the likelihood of the firm being on the hook for those costs if something goes awry? If you have taken an introductory economics course, you're familiar with the concept of "opportunity costs," namely, the value of what you're giving up in order to pursue something potentially lucrative. When you're trying to determine the appropriate billing arrangement for a new client, you need to consider the opportunity cost of taking on a given client or matter. In other words, you'll need to compare what you are giving up—both tangible and current opportunities as well as hypothetical opportunities in the future—with the opportunity to profit from the current client matter. What other activities will the firm give up, such as marketing and client outreach, in order to take on the matter or to cultivate long-term growth? Every moment you spend on the phone engaging with a client about his concern will be time that you won't have to spend researching or reaching out to other potential clients with possibly lucrative matters of their own.

As for the external billing inputs, start by considering the interests of your clients; client-side factors will dictate what will be an appropriate billing arrangement. Some companies might need to work with you on an hourly basis only, while other clients might balk at that. Monthly fees may work well for your larger clients whose legal needs are more sophisticated and less predictable. You will also need to determine who it is that is actually paying for your services. Whose bank account is the money actually coming from? Sure, you are working for a small privately held company, but if that company is being funded primarily by one of the LLC members or shareholders, then that individual is the one paying for your services. You should know who that is.

Thus, in addition, you cannot simply consider the prospects and billing aptitude of the company; you must also consider those of the key players. For example, if the CEO of your client company were to strike it rich with the business, but otherwise has limited experience in business and prefers to spend his time flying between NY and LA to visit his girlfriends, you might be wise to think twice about assigning a high value to his client matter and its future revenue. On the other hand, if that key individual has a 25-year career in healthcare, enjoys strong family and community ties, and is motivated by more than just quick ways to generate discretionary income, he may be worth a larger gamble of your firm's time and resources.

Here's another externally focused question to ask yourself: where would the money for the company's legal fees go, if not to you? Who is foregoing additional income in order to pay your fees? If there are shareholders who are agreeing to pay your fees, then you need to consider their temperaments, too. How much of the budget is going to pay for your fees? Will it result in a noticeable decrease in their quarterly distributions? How is one of these shareholders likely to evaluate the rationale for paying you? Does one of those shareholders dislike your firm because of a dispute his wife had with one of your cousin's best friends? Does another feel that your firm should have been a sponsor to his charity's umpteenth fund-raising gala of the year? These examples may seem comical but be assured these types of dynamics are always at play in a service business, especially when you are in a relatively small business niche where everybody knows everybody. It happens when you're dealing with small to mid-sized companies that haven't adopted a stiff formal corporate culture. But these dynamics can also be found within the highest echelons of corporate and legal. It will just take time and effort to effectively sift through the many layers and organizational detritus to arrive at the information. So it behooves the small, independent firm to be especially sensitive to all of the dynamics at play with the key individuals who control a large client's decisions to pay your legal fees.

The best strategy to maximize your value proposition is to arrive at an accurate assessment of a potential client's ability to pay as well as their long-term solvency and their interests motivating their decision to hire an attorney. Then consider your fee and payment options, consider the impact on your firm, and offer what makes the most sense for that particular client. With a clear commitment and terms for payment, you will establish comfortable revenues that will grow surprisingly quickly.

## PLANNING AHEAD

Setting your rates and fees at your small law practice is a balancing act; it's an art, not a science. On the one hand, you don't want to look unsophisticated by pricing too cheaply, yet you want to price competitively to get the job. On the other, you don't want to make your initial payment proposal too high, lest you offend the prospect and sour the relationship. To find the sweet spot, you have to weigh a variety of factors to gauge and price according to your client's needs, expectations, and their ability to pay. You'll also consider their appetite for legal fees as well as their prior experience with other firms and attorneys. Some clients don't blink at paying

$50,000–100,000 monthly while others would walk out the door if you suggested it.

When planning a billing strategy, it is very helpful to have a partner to discuss it with. As a firm that generally eschews many of the formalities, our new matter billing discussions are some of our most structured. The two of us consistently have in-depth conversations to plan our billing strategy—both short and long term. Each partner will describe what billing inputs they feel are significant, both those that are internal to the firm and those that relate to the prospective client. While we're discussing our views, different things about the situation jump out as significant to one partner or the other. It has also been incredibly valuable to discuss these openly with a particular client and come to a consensus about the strategy we choose to take with them. Not being on the same page as your partner(s) about your long-term billing strategy has the potential to lead to crippling conflict. If one partner views a client as not worthwhile for the firm, while another partner loves the work and thinks it's a great opportunity, the disagreement can cause problems that could damage the relationship and eventually the firm.

You'll find that some companies come to you already holding a dislike for lawyers because of a negative experience they've had in the past. In the back of their minds, they wonder if they should go somewhere else, if they are paying too much, or if they don't actually need a lawyer. But if you've built an expertise in a niche as we discussed in the last chapter, if your services are excellent, and if you set your fees such that they are appropriate to their needs and ability to pay, you can win them over for the long term.

Then, once you establish your expertise in your business niche, you'll have many fewer clients who are only "window-shopping" for attorneys. They'll be less likely to constantly think about switching firms—as many clients often do—and they'll be less susceptible to other firms' sales pitches while you have their business. One key reason they have chosen your firm is because they think they have found the best fit for their business. They have not chosen based solely on compensation arrangements. Your ability to adapt to their needs when deciding payment arrangements is an added bonus for them—the cherry on top.

Your positioning within your business niche also buys you a lot when it comes to having those inevitable conversations you have with your clients about billing. Because you provide a unique and valuable service in a world that has rather few substitutes, you have a stronger bargaining position than you otherwise would have. Your clients will have to acknowledge that any other firm won't provide the perfect fit as you do, since there are so few out there that can match your niche expertise. When it's time to negotiating billing, you can emphasize your firm's extensive understanding of their business and your unique value to them, which few other attorneys could claim. They're looking for someone just like you and they know it.

Be sure to factor in the experience and temperament of the people with whom you're working out the actual payment arrangements. Typically, you're negotiating with one, two, or three people who are making the decisions. Some businesses have experienced people making their financial arrangements who know how to avoid paying for legal fees whenever they can. They'll balk at any type of flat monthly fee arrangement if they think they're capable of avoiding some legal fees or hidden costs. Also consider their past experience with attorneys. It might be good to ask them questions about their past relationships and what worked and didn't work for them regarding billing. These insights can provide valuable information to your billing strategy.

Then make sure that you balance this tactic against the risk of encountering a firm that wants to squeeze free work out of you. Some—often younger, less experienced business executives—will try hard to get their legal matter handled for free. They might want forms for free, or your opinions and conclusions about a matter, for free. Depending on their particular experience, their incentives and budgets, some general counsel can often be more like chief legal cost cutters, rather than proactive attorneys responsible for leading a robust legal strategy. They have a roster of small firms or independent lawyers to call on for the next one in line for their endless string of favors. Watch out and learn to recognize these people to avoid wasting your time on them.

Some organizations just happen to be very good at keeping their legal needs to a minimum. These clients may still prove profitable to your firm over a long relationship. Steady, reliable income for a small independent law firm is not to be underestimated. It can prove to play a critical role in the progress of your firm as you invest in more long-term business niche expertise or client development. In these cases, your billing calculus needs to make a realistic fee proposal. Your flat fee retainer could easily be a fraction of what a large law firm would try to charge.

Once you've completed the information-gathering process described above and the accompanying analysis, then and only then it is time to begin talking to your client for the purpose of negotiating your desired billing arrangement.

## OPEN COMMUNICATION

The value of communicating with your clients with regard to your firm's billing arrangement cannot be overstressed. Good communication creates a foundation of trust and allows you to respond to their unique needs so they value you for the long term. It starts with your first meeting.

Right from the start, work to establish good rapport with your potential clients. Save the billing arrangement discussion for later. Spend a couple of hours talking about their issues and their interests, and recognize the difference between the two. A client may come to you with a discrete legal issue, but to maximize your ability to serve their legal needs you will also need to understand the client interests that lie behind it. For a basic example, consider the assignment of reviewing a vendor contract. Does the client want you to review to ensure they are not committing to too much, that the agreement meets regulatory requirements, that the agreement "locks in" the other side? Moreover, where does this particular vendor relationship rank in the priority of the firm? Are there many others out there who could take this role, or is this a mission-critical agreement for the firm? Do the next few quarters of profit depend on the outcome of this vendor contract negotiation? Focus on their concerns and listen to them to understand what matters most to them. Then, at the right time, make a point of mentioning the flexibility of your billing arrangements without making it the main point of the conversation. Let them know that you'd be happy to be flexible with them so you can come up with an ideal arrangement, whether it's an hourly fee or a flat monthly retainer. Let them know that you will do what's best for them.

Then, near the end of the meeting, reprise the basics of the financial conversation. Emphasize that your pricing is competitive, in fact much cheaper than others. Remind them of your expertise in their world: their business. But save the substantive billing proposal and negotiations for another, second conversation. You want the client thinking about legal solutions and the value you can add to their operation, not about how they are going to be able to afford you. This two-step process also allows you additional time to review, discuss, and plan your billing strategy based on your in-depth conversation and incorporate any direct or indirect feedback you receive. It should be clear at this point that the "negotiation" of a billing arrangement involves much more time spent gathering information, analyzing, and planning, than in the actual communication with the client.

Since you've done your homework and listened to your client, when it's time to make a proposal, you line it right up with your prospective client's expectations and needs. You could even spell it out for them. Make it easy for them to sign with you by saying, "You know, Jeri, you don't have any litigations going on, your agreements are done. You might have ongoing regulatory issues that come up, but you don't need 'round the clock attorneys at your disposal." Then you could propose a flat monthly fee arrangement, for example, that's lower than what the bigger companies would offer yet more aligned with what your client wants. Help them clearly see the benefits of working with you by informing them of the rates the work would normally be billed at, and giving them a ballpark rate. Then reveal the sweet deal you're offering. When you frame the negotiation in terms of your clients' interests and external factors, instead of how much you need to bill them to pay for your overhead and still represent them, you're going to get a much better response. We've acquired a few former BigLaw clients doing just that.

Over the months and years that you work with your clients, make a practice of calling them even if you don't have a pressing legal issue that needs to be reviewed. Check in and ask how the business is doing, where they are going, and what obstacles they are currently facing. Ask how they feel about your relationship with them. Is there anything that your firm can be helpful with? These types of conversations also make it easier to talk about billing when you need to go there. You've established rapport before issues arise and you've shown that you care about their needs; you don't just call when you need to discuss bills and payment.

Also, review your existing and past billing arrangements for data to use in future billing negotiations. If an arrangement is judged ex post to be a poor one, what made it so poor? Did the arrangement end up involving too much work for the price? Too little work so that the client grew upset? Would hourly have been more fair than the flat fee? Keep handy notes on these to remember for the future.

## PRICE DISCRIMINATION

At a large law firm, pricing for legal services is often set in stone and rigidly adhered to, mainly owing to the internal billing inputs of a large law firm. But as a small company—legal or otherwise—it can be a wise strategy to be able to vary the pricing structure for the same service depending upon the scope of the work and what works best for your new client. You're the emerging talent, so you want to offer better services at better prices. In many situations, you might want to adjust the hourly fee, negotiate the up-front retainer, or offer a lower flat fee arrangement.

You could say that the airline industry uses this approach on a broad scale. They'll charge at one level for services to business customers and another level for consumer travel. Business travelers often travel out of necessity; their employer pays for their flight and expects them to be alert and well rested upon arrival. The demand for business class travel has become quite insensitive to changes in price, and remains dictated by the needs of the business, so an airline can offer almost any fare it chooses. Vacation travelers face greater price sensitivity, so their market for airplane tickets has become very competitive. This explains why business class seats can cost more than ten times the price of a coach ticket. Airlines also vary their prices based on when a ticket is purchased, the date of travel (whether vacation season or "down time") and the quantity of tickets bought. All of these strategies serve to maximize the profits of the airlines with relatively little outcry from consumers who allege these practices are unfair or unreasonable. A similar strategy is available to you as a small, flexible, independent law firm, especially one who has relative expertise in a particular business niche.

The most obvious opportunity for law firm price discrimination is to charge wealthier clients, who have a greater ability to pay, higher fees. While on its face this can be a beneficial strategy, recall that the client's ability to pay is just one of many billing inputs that your firm must consider when developing a billing arrangement. Additionally, if you have chosen a smaller business niche within which to develop your expertise, be mindful that smaller industries spread information more easily. Clients often communicate with peers in their industry, so your legal fees may become public knowledge to other current or potential clients.

Keep in mind that a client's ability to pay can also involve a temporal element: clients with deep pockets today may or may not have those deep pockets six months from now, a year from now, or five years from now. Clients also didn't get to be successful by overpaying for things. They will learn rather quickly if they are paying too much for your services. We saw that dynamic first hand. On the other hand, the ones that are likely to have large financial resources well into the future can present an opportunity for greater profits and a longer-term relationship with your law firm.

We have seen first-hand the BigLaw tendency to "get their fees" from a big client as quickly as possible. They take over the lawsuit and unleash a flurry of litigation activity for two months, only to get cut off by the client when they get their second monthly legal bill in the six figures. A much more reasonable approach, especially for a small firm, would be to establish a sustainable baseline and make the client comfortable with the ebbs and flows of litigation, without gouging them out of your services. Sixteen months of five-figure fees amounts to a lot more than five months of six-figure fees, assuming you expect your firm to be around in 16 months.

You may actually decide to charge the newer, developing clients a little more to get started than you do the larger companies. While it seems counterintuitive, you can provide complimentary or discounted services to your more established clients but charge full price to your smaller client for the same work. For example, drawing up formation or other documents might be a throw-away to a large company, and hardly worth charging for in comparison with the rest of the work you'll do for them. But that work may be the sole reason why a new startup wants to engage you.

As we mentioned before, sometimes problem clients can dominate your time or resources. Remember, you have the option to charge a higher flat fee to clients who are more difficult and high-maintenance. They're the ones who call you any time of day, often challenging your legal expertise with novel business ideas, and constantly asking you to hop on a call or a flight on the spur of the moment to meet a new potential business partner. That's worth the extra fees. Sometimes having the conversation about fees and potential cost increases can be a not-so-subtle way to say, "Stop calling me so much for such non-important discussions."

## HOURLY VS. FLAT FEES

Every business is unique. If a smaller business, such as a small physician practice, manages its finances and operations correctly, it probably won't warrant large monthly legal fees; a reasonable hourly rate, or even a flat, per-project fee, will likely suit them best. On the other hand, unexpected issues will sometimes come up and the client will keep calling you for more work if they value your services. So you both win.

Larger companies will often have lots of work for you as well as unexpected legal issues that arise frequently. You are likely to be called on to devote significant resources to the issue. Larger organizations also have sophisticated budgeting processes and often want a flat fee arrangement to manage their cash flow risk. That becomes more important to them than reducing nominal costs.

Hourly billing can be very attractive to new clients and easy for you to manage, but it does carry a cost. Preparing hourly billing statements complete with detailed descriptions of the work for each hourly increment takes a lot of time. The time you spend doing time sheets might be better spent doing other substantive work on legal matters, administration, or even leisure.

However, some matters require detailed time keeping anyway, reducing the weight of this issue on the scales of your decision making. For example, in bankruptcy cases, you have to account for your hours and get your fees approved by the court anyway. In litigated cases, where legal fees are being claimed against the other side, you'll still have to make the effort to track your time.

Still, some attorneys don't like flat fee arrangements because it changes their attitude too much when they do their legal work. If you choose to adopt a flat fee payment arrangement, you may have to adjust your mindset to ensure you are maintaining the quality of your efforts even though each additional hour of work does not equal an additional fee. Frankly, some attorneys are simply not psychologically capable of maintaining their standards without the marginal revenue motivation. Be aware of where you fall on this continuum and adjust accordingly. The tendency is always a risk, and you need to monitor yourself to avoid this potentially unethical behavior. The last thing your firm wants is a reputation for taking monthly fees from clients while doing the minimum amount of work.

While you start some companies at an hourly rate, you can keep an eye out for the right time to move them into a monthly flat fee arrangement. The switch can be very effective if you are listening to your client and sense some dissatisfaction or strain on their ability to pay, perhaps owing to outside forces. Often these conversations can prompt the client to take stock of their legal needs and communicate new issues they need resolved, but have for whatever reason hesitated to ask you to explore just yet. Discussing how you want to make sure they're happy with the billing arrangement can be a good way to remind them they have a lot more work for you to do.

Fairness sometimes requires that you take your medicine, too. If you go with flat fees, you do have to monitor yourself and be vigilant about continuing to provide excellent services even if the marginal value of each additional hour of work is decreasing for you or your firm. In other words, you need to be comfortable even when you have a month when your firm chalks up a net loss and does much more work than the value of your monthly fee. It's the arrangement you've agreed to, so you can only learn from it for future negotiations.

## RETAINERS

Notwithstanding our commitment to billing flexibility and our espousing of it as a highly beneficial practice, we do require upfront retainers for new clients even when we're billing hourly. Retainers act as a down payment on the work to be performed and are applied toward the total fee billed. The funds in the retainer are typically used to pay the first month's invoice and need to be large enough at least to cover anticipated work and expenses to the end of that billing period. Charging a retainer lets you mitigate your risk and prevents your firm from being at the bad end of the effect of a client's financial status or changes of mind.

We highly recommend retainers for every firm for every new client. They serve as a real and abstract gesture of commitment by your client and signal that the client agrees that they must pay you for your services. Obviously, retainers also provide security for your firm, in case the relationship sours. That said, we did have one experience in which we felt it best to return the retainer, minus fees actually billed. The client was a consulting company that had many contacts throughout our industry. We wanted to preserve our reputation and avoid as much potential ill will as possible stemming from the soured relationship. So we took care of ourselves on both sides of the arrangement.

While the vast majority of lawyers require large retainers, we don't ask for much. Many large firms measure their success on how big a retainer they can score but our experience has taught us that the amount of money that actually comes into the bank account during and after your engagement is much more important. Since you're your own boss, you don't have to impress your superiors with the money you brought in on retainers and you're not focused on making your profit on the retainer. While it does offer risk management, its effect is really more symbolic. It's more about establishing trust and buy-in from the client through approval and commitment to the billing arrangement than about the actual revenue. Be reasonable and flexible: it will work to your advantage in the long run. Again, we think of our clients first—both to make them happy and to build our business.

If you decide that charging a retainer is the way to go with a client, your challenge once again will be to find the sweet spot for the charge. You want to gain an advantage from your competition by offering lower rates, but if you set them too low, you'll sabotage your credibility. You want to get paid fairly and you want to signal that you're a legitimate law firm, but you don't want to price yourself out of business. If it's at an appropriate level, you're signaling that your rates are commensurate with you being a sophisticated, legitimate, and credible law firm.

When our firm was just getting started, we were negotiating with a prospective company that we really wanted to win over, so we didn't want to price our proposal out of their range. We chose to propose a relatively low, accessible upfront retainer and hourly fee combination. They turned us down almost immediately. When we inquired about what happened, they told us that the low figures gave them the strong impression that we must not be very sophisticated, talented, or capable—and they decided to look elsewhere.

We've never made that mistake again.

Setting your rates too high can also be an issue, but as long as you provide a discount from what the large law firms in your city are offering, you probably won't find your opening billing proposal to be a deal breaker that ends the conversation. Even though you're setting yourself apart by specializing in your business niche, you always want to provide a discount on the big all-purpose firms that your clients might have experience with or are currently evaluating. If your fees are too close to those large firm fees, you may not be able to justify the "perceived" reduction in availability. After all, as a small firm, you won't be able to provide all the services a big firm can provide. Even if you think you can, your client will likely feel that way. And their perception is what feeds their decision to work with you or not.

If you think we are speaking out of both sides of our mouths and not giving you a concrete formula, you're right. This is an art, not a science. Many factors go into these decisions, but at the end of the day, it's a case-by-case determination. And you get better over time. The point is to use these experiences and lessons as a guide in your early billing arrangement determination process. You'll have to gain true expertise through your own experience.

## HOW TO NAVIGATE LATE PAYMENTS AND FAILURE TO PAY

There's a widespread assumption among law firms that if you don't get paid on time then you should immediately stop providing any further legal services. This may work fine for BigLaw firms who can afford to abandon clients at will. But if you're a small firm and you have the insight to understand the businesses you work with, you can offer more flexibility that other firms might not be willing or capable of and it will pay off in the long term. You can work out arrangements with organizations based on their needs and capabilities, and give them a little longer to make payments where larger law firms would not be willing or able to. We can afford to do this because we keep our overhead super low. That means we don't feel pressured to get immediate cash flow. We are not talking about taking out loans for big swings in revenue and profit. We are not speculators. There are some successful law firms that follow this model and operate like this—mainly big plaintiffs' firms. But that is not our business niche model and so we won't address those tactics in detail. It's the same for you: you can afford to wait since you're a small, flexible firm on its way up. So give your clients the extra time if they need it. When you do, you get to keep the client, build more trust, be the hero, and get paid in full.

Again, good communication and listening to your client pays you back in the end. By understanding their situation and their needs, you can navigate late payments in a way that serves them and keeps them coming back.

As a side note, according to tax advice we received from our accountant, we are not able to write off unpaid legal fees for work that was actually performed. So don't think you are doing yourself any favors by providing write-offs—it is simply lost productivity no matter how you slice it.

We were working with a large laboratory client a couple of years ago that found itself in the middle of a business downturn largely owing to the faulty billing practices of another company that they were working with. They were facing a suspension from participating in a healthcare billing program that represented a significant portion of their company's revenue and their financial systems were in terrible disarray. We understood their business well enough and we understood what was happening to them, so we felt comfortable with not getting payments from them for two to three months. But anyone we mentioned this to told us we were crazy. "Why would you do one ounce of legal work for anybody without money up front?" they asked. They insisted that we should stop working for them at once. But we thought, no, we are convinced that they're going to be fine. We knew the new billing company they hired and felt confident that they'd get their billing issue worked out. Again, it is worth noting that we were not borrowing money to float this cash flow disruption. We had other clients and other matters enabling us to keep the lights on.

Because we had established a good working relationship with them, we knew the client well. They were controlled and run by an individual with 25+ years of business experience in the same state.

He had slowly built up his practice over the years and had established extensive ties to the community. He articulated to us a robust plan for fighting the suspension and weathering the storm while continuing to operate. We knew he was not a fly-by-night venture, speculating on a temporarily attractive business, that would abandon ship once the going got tough. So we kept on performing our legal services and eventually we were paid in full for our work. They've remained with us as very loyal clients.

While we talk up flexibility, we also recognize that there's also a limit to it. When a client contacts us with a concern about their ability to pay a bill, we will not negotiate or reduce what is owed. We resist all attempts to discount. As discussed above, you can signal your flexibility and empathy by allowing more time to pay past due amounts, yet remain true to your firm's financial interests by not reducing or discounting. After all, it's much better to be paid late than to be paid less. And the client agreed to pay. It's a lot easier to pursue the full amount in either bankruptcy or litigation (heaven forbid) without having to explain away attempts at good faith discounts. Here again, communication is key. Listen closely to what the client has to say—and what they don't say—and use your best judgment. Notice if the company is not paying some people—as their attorney, you will likely learn about that pretty soon. Consider who is not getting paid and why. It may not be doomsday if some nonessential vendors are paid late, but if they're not paying their rent, it could easily mean the walls are coming down, literally and figuratively. If so, it's time to get what you can and consider ending the relationship.

It is important to be proactive. Clients are very busy people and they need to be reminded they owe money. They get hundreds of emails every day and in any month they are juggling hundreds of invoices. Maybe they don't have a sophisticated accounts payable department; sometimes things fall through the cracks. So be sure to be prompt with your payment reminders. If a payment shows up late, then call them up and have a conversation with them as soon as possible. If you wait three months, you won't have much leverage to get paid anymore, so be proactive and get on top of it right away. Send warnings to any client in need of risk management.

In fact, we have clients who depend on our monthly invoices to remind them of the balance due and to help them with their budgeting purposes. We've had some get very upset at us when we went for three months without invoicing them and then hit them with a big bill. It serves them for us to be on top of it.

We rarely threaten to withdraw owing to payment issues—unless we mean it. You don't want to scare anyone off. If you do, they get desperate and you both lose. Instead, manage their payment schedule.

## PLANNING FOR POTENTIAL WITHDRAWAL

As flexible as we are in negotiating billing arrangements with our clients, we have our limits. As mentioned, we don't waive fees or forgive what is owed, and we recommend that you don't either.

Even before you take on a case or a client, consider the possibility that you may need to eventually withdraw for billing or other reasons. Some states make it difficult for a law firm to withdraw simply for nonpayment of fees. Some courts can weigh several factors when they consider whether withdrawing from the matter is permitted, including the firm's diligence, their potential prejudice to the client, the financial impact of the firm on doing the case without payment, and so forth. This implies that a court may also look at the reasonableness of fees due and fees already paid. So be sure to communicate these considerations clearly to your potential client each step along the way as you negotiate fees. You don't want to be in a position before the court, looking like you are just raising the issue to defend your desire to withdraw and to convince the court after your client stopped paying.

We were working with a company that found itself needing to go through bankruptcy reorganization. They wanted to keep us as counsel because of our laboratory expertise, but we didn't know the new management very well. Another, larger firm, which had its own "healthcare" practice group, was handling the reorganization. While we had the trust of some of the client's decision makers, we faced the inevitable prospect of having to justify our fees to the bankruptcy court. That meant we had to justify our fees to the law firm who was in charge of the process and in more control of communication with the bankruptcy court, which meant we would likely have other attorneys looking over our shoulders. These types of dynamics require strategic thinking and additional, non-billable time and effort to make sure our firm didn't get the end around. On top of that, we would inevitably have to reduce our fees to bring them in line with the strictures of the reorganization plan. After enduring a few substantive and difficult conversations regarding the client, we decided not to continue. We could have made some money, but at what cost? The company would not survive bankruptcy, liquidation was inevitable, so there was no long-term relationship in play. It was not in the long-term best interests of our firm; the cost of maintaining that revenue was too high.

## PROACTIVE BILLING

It's absolutely essential that you bill your clients consistently, at least every month. Small firms without a sophisticated and well-staffed billing department have a big tendency to fall behind on billing and invoicing. But you'll find that many companies, especially those that are small and have volatile cash flow concerns, will get very upset if you send an invoice that reflects four months of legal services, regardless if they have already used you before and paid regularly for several months. Many businesses track cash flow by the invoices they receive so if you submit an invoice for four prior months, it can throw off their budgeting system and can lead to significant displeasure, even if payment would not have been an issue if they were budgeting consistently. It's wise, therefore, and to your advantage to avoid these unnecessary discomforts by using consistent billing practices.

For many of your larger business clients with sophisticated, complex legal issues, you're basically setting yourself up as their on-call lawyer. These are the ones that pay the most and therefore are at greatest risk if their accounts receivable aren't able to be collected. The answer to this is that you need to plan for it. Likewise, you might have a client that goes bankrupt. Whether or not you can't collect, the faucet might get shut off right away, so you need to plan for that situation too. But as their attorney, you are often very well apprised of a company's financial circumstances. You know where they stand. When you know that they are good for it, you can work out an arrangement that is suitable to you both. You just need to plan for it. (By the way, if you are considering representing a company that is going through a bankruptcy proceeding, your fees are subject to court-mandated reduction.)

As you may have gathered, there is no well-defined billing formula. There is no silver bullet. Law firm billing is best considered an art rather than a science. And there is no one-size-fits-all model for knowing how much and how to charge your clients. But by adhering to the three principles of flexibility, communication, and planning, our firm has developed what we feel is a superior ability to create billing arrangements that bring about the long-term benefit of our firm as well as our clients. By focusing on the client's interests first and foremost, we have developed a reputation for fair billing practices and have kept the focus on our exemplary services and expertise. We have been fortunate to build sustainable relationships in sometimes volatile business environments where other firms adopting traditional strategies would not have fared as well. While your firm's billing inputs and your clients' billing inputs will necessarily differ from ours, you can use the strategies outlined in this chapter to craft superior, sustainable billing practices.

In the next chapter, we will share the best practices we have found for hiring and managing staff and by doing so, supported the healthy growth of our law firm.

# 6. Staffing a small firm

The hiring and managing processes that will be advantageous for a smaller, independent firm are going to be different from those at large, established law firms who have hundreds of employees, deep pockets, and highly structured environments. The latter are well suited to the business objectives and bottom-line concerns of those large firms. But when it comes to launching a small firm, the focus needs to be on maximizing flexibility, minimizing costs, developing a sustainable organizational structure, establishing a business culture, and—let's be honest—getting through the first few lean months.

In this chapter, we'll walk you through the human capital and staffing principles that have helped keep our business moving upward and onward when we were establishing our niche practice and making a name for ourselves. The principles are divided into two main categories: hiring and managing. When we talk of hiring, we'll talk about the importance of not rushing your growth, contingency planning, and a few other helpful practices for hiring. We'll talk about identifying and evaluating your firm culture—and allowing that culture to inform your hiring decisions. When we discuss management, we'll focus on managing expectations and incentives, and how we believe that most, if not all, decisions and activities thought of as "management" comprise one or both of them. The purpose of this chapter is not to try to provide a scientific analysis or arrive at a seemingly scientific method; we do not assume to provide the ultimate authority on law firm staffing or management. Rather, we are sharing our experience and the lessons we've learned to help you improve your odds of success as you develop your business niche law practice.

# GOING SOLO

Like almost anyone who launches a new small business, you're probably going to have to work long hours in the beginning, wear a lot of hats, and do a lot of the work yourself. The question soon dawns: when should you start hiring, and how many do you hire? The first few months of business is the time to keep expenses to a minimum, slowly evolve the organizational structure, and craft, learn, and master the administrative functions and business operations of your firm. It's best not to burden yourself with the large and complex demands of managing a lot of employees while you're still establishing your business infrastructure.

Real-life history has demonstrated that many small firms, while wanting to have the depth of resources they need to respond to incoming business, make the mistake of hiring too many people too early and expecting business to simply come knocking on their door. But that approach can backfire by putting unnecessary pressure on the firm and the new hires and can cause harmful effects by disturbing the company morale and culture. If you build it, they won't necessarily come. The lesson is: don't hire to build capacity for a firm. If you cannot bring in the business yourselves then you have no business hiring more lawyers yet.

Quite the contrary, the approach we took was to bring in the business first and try to be creative and flexible in hiring practices while our business grew. In fact, as a smaller, independent firm, we were in an optimal position to "go to where the clients are" for two reasons. First, as a small firm, we had the dexterity to try new approaches and take business risks. And second, business niche specialization allowed us to ignore geographical considerations and capture business far beyond our local area. We started with a couple of clients in Atlanta, Georgia, for example, but now have clients in Utah, Colorado, Israel, San Antonio, and beyond. Remaining a small and agile company for a while worked to our advantage as we built our name, our experience, and our business.

# HIRING CONTRACTORS AND INTERNS

When it's time to start bringing employees into your ranks, we recommend you begin by hiring contractors and interns to keep your payroll costs as slim as possible. Especially in our early stages of development, we hired a number of associates on a part-time or contract basis. We wouldn't have our practice today if we had done otherwise. For a small firm just getting started, these are some of the lowest-risk hires you'll have available to you since neither you nor they have any expectations that the work or the position will continue for any length of time. At the same time, there's always the possibility that more matters will arise for them to take on, and it might end up leading to actual full-time hires, if you're ready to go there.

Think about it. There are plenty of lawyers available who would be happy to make some extra money and get some work that might lead to full-time employment. Don't believe us? Look on indeed. com or even craigslist. Check out your local law school's alumni career site (if they have one). Across the country, thousands of lawyers who already have jobs have their names out for a better position, not to mention the thousands of others who are fully in the job market. Some are fresh out of law school, others are under-employed graduates who have extra time and want to make more income. Some are BigLaw veterans who'd like to be there as their child grows up in real life—not staring at a Skype screen while the nanny tucks the child in for bed. These lawyers have real-world skills. And as a smaller firm, you have the time and the dexterity to spend more time sussing out their legal capabilities beyond just reading their resume, judging them by their law school, or determining whether or not they "made it" to BigLaw. If your preference is to get the job done quickly and cost-effectively, while minimizing lock-in effects and commitment from hiring, then going with contractors is a great option.

We hired contractors as needed to help with specific matters we had on our roster. We took on a seasoned litigator, for example, to help us with a very large corporate litigation. He had left his BigLaw firm to go to business school and he had time and experience to be very instrumental to our success with the matter. There are active lawyers everywhere who have low-paying 9–5 jobs and time on their hands who are looking for more work. People have all sorts of reasons for needing the additional income. New baby. New house. Old debts. They come ready and willing to work for you under more flexible terms than full-time employees.

Where do you find lawyers looking for contract work? Start with friends. Your law school friends, friends of friends, and friends of family are all good referral sources. They might not end up working out for the long term, but they can get some quality work done for you if you choose wisely. Another way to look at it, too, is that since you haven't invested much in the way of time and training beyond the specific matter you give them, they are not that costly for you to lose.

We insist on being upfront about the potentially fleeting nature of the line of work we're in. A break in the case, a change in the strategy, or a hit to the client's ability to pay their bills could all mean that the gig is no longer profitable for the firm. Despite how difficult it may seem at the time, employee expenses can be cut relatively quickly, so if you need to trim expenses, don't hesitate to do so. If you have managed expectations with the contractor regarding the nature of the engagement upfront, there should be no hard feelings. At the same time, you can't control another person's feelings, so don't feel bad if there is some tension; you can be confident that you behaved fairly within the context of the engagement.

Another benefit of working with these attorneys is that they can work remotely on their off hours. But this arrangement has its limitations, too, which we'll discuss later in this chapter.

You can also get great help from law students *before* they graduate. We have hired several outstanding interns from law schools. They're smart, they're hungry, and they are motivated like no one else because the job market (still) sucks and there are very few full-time positions available. This type of experience is invaluable for competing for those sought-after BigLaw positions, if that is their ultimate goal. They are paid relatively well, too, for where they are in life, and they'll get great material for their resume that they probably couldn't get anywhere else. To our firm, the $20–30/ hour cost was very attractive compared with our alternatives.

University externship programs are a great place to look for student interns. Law schools are usually very happy to hear from you because many want to incorporate more of an apprenticeship model so that their students can get some real-life experience. If you have one in your area, track down the professors in the Law Department and ask them for recommendations for part-time help. Here in Atlanta, Georgia, we've had great results working with the

Emory Law University's Externship Program as well as with the Georgia State Law School's Healthcare Law Program. Emory likes giving their students the feel for small law and we find that Georgia State likes the arrangement because it supports their academic program with practical, hands-on healthcare law experience.

Of course, there are limitations to the advantages of working with student interns. We learned that we needed to come up with discrete assignments; it was sometimes tough to give them long-term, complex cases. We realized that we couldn't call on them whenever we wanted to. Sometimes their assignments needed to be completed more quickly than expected, like when the deadline suddenly moved up and we needed it "now", not next week. And it was sometimes a challenge to generate discrete, "intern-friendly" assignments when the list of the firm's current matters had gotten short. When we had some lulls in activity for the interns, we put them to work developing the internal knowledge base of the firm.

As we developed our business niche practice using the methods described in this book, tricky legal research questions would frequently arise that were important but tangential to the actual assignments at hand. We wanted to delve into this research question or that, and perhaps discover some facts that could help one or more of our matters or open up an opportunity for our clients—if only we had the time. With interns on hand, we had that time: their time. We put our interns to work on those types of research assignments. They can learn and they will contribute to the firm's expertise. Hiring student interns is a great, cheap supplement to your hiring and staffing practices that a solo practitioner or large firm would never consider.

We also learned not to scoff at the potential contribution of interns or very junior level employees; they can sometimes make the critical difference in a given matter. Early in our firm's history, an intern (and later, employee) played a crucial role in helping us win a large litigation case for one of our biggest clients. The case was an unfair competition case between two laboratories in Florida. A plaintiff's attorney had convinced himself that he could represent a laboratory and go after a rival laboratory based on alleged violations of Florida and federal healthcare fraud and abuse statutes, using Florida's Unfair and Deceptive Trade Practices Act. While there was some precedent informing this attorney that his might be a viable strategy, he was ultimately bogged down in the complexity of laboratory operations and regulations, of which he had no previous experience. Our firm took over the case and counter-sued as we gathered evidence that the plaintiff laboratory was engaged in similar conduct. We dug in for a fight.

It turned out that the plaintiff had sued in Florida business court, a special court in the state of Florida that was designed to streamline business disputes. The judges in the court move cases quickly with monthly telephone call hearings and a special set of procedural rules apply to proceedings. Although we had local counsel, since we were in uncharted territories, we tasked our intern with reviewing and summarizing the business court rules.

At the point at which we took over the case, our side had not conducted any depositions, while the plaintiff had administered several depositions of sales employees—customers of our client— and seemed to be scheduling a new deposition every day. This was, understandably, causing our client a ton of anxiety and lost productivity. The other side had yet to depose the principal witnesses: the owners/officers of our client company. But lo and behold, while conducting the review of the business court rules, our intern discovered that each side is limited to 10 depositions only, barring extreme circumstances. It was a huge breakthrough for our side: we could shut down the plaintiff's harassing discovery. We immediately moved for a protective order against any further depositions. The plaintiff was broken. Within a few weeks the case ended.

## USING LOCAL COUNSEL

Given the nature of our business niche practice, we are often presented with both the opportunities and the challenges of handling matters in states outside of where attorneys in our firm are licensed. When considering whether to accept an assignment, you'll want to factor in how much additional cost will be borne to your firm and to your client, and the impact that declining the matter might have on your relationship with them. The immediate reaction is that you never want another firm looking over your shoulder or handling a matter side by side with you. Fact is, clients often expect that their law firm can handle any matter; after all, that is one of the selling points of your business niche expertise. So we found that a successful business niche practice will involve utilizing the services of local counsel.

Many attorneys all over the country are capable and willing of handling a Pro Hac Vice arrangement. This is an art in and of itself and it supports you in your efforts to hire slow. (It's curious to us how we never heard the phrase *Pro Hac Vice* uttered even once in law school.) The beauty of it is that you don't need to hire a Utah lawyer if you want to handle a client or a case that's based in Utah. Working with an attorney Pro Hac Vice means that he or she knows the local rules and quirks in the local litigation system. They vouch to the court that they will oversee your handling of the matter and actually sign each of the briefs and pleadings that you submit. It's also helpful if they are familiar with the court and the judges in the area. Even better is when your local counsel's daughter is a college roommate with the son of the federal judge who is deciding your motion to dismiss. That really happened to us!

But, as with anything, there are risks when it comes to Pro Hac Vice arrangements. The biggest risk isn't that they won't be competent enough—actually some of the best local counsel for your purposes are the *least* competent. The biggest risk is that they are *too* competent and might attempt to hijack your matter or your client by dazzling them or sinking their teeth into elements of the case that give them the "lead role." We've seen various tactics used to employ this strategy on several matters. One of the most common tactics is to use their supposedly "inside" knowledge of local players to convince the client that they need to be the lead attorney. To counter, we ask why can't they just show up for hearings to have superficial face time with whatever judge they want to ingratiate themselves with? Another tactic is to amp up the complexity of the matter. Inevitably the complexity involves local discovery rules that only they can adequately handle for the client, and only adequately handle as lead counsel.

We've actually seen a local counsel try to claim to our client that the case would be won or lost on discovery related only to jurisdiction, and that the client needed to go all in with their firm (at a healthy five to six figure monthly cost of course). The eventual outcome was that our motion to dismiss, which our firm drafted, kicked the case out. Then we immediately re-filed in the client's home state, whose federal case law was much more friendly to our side. Tough luck for the jurisdictional discovery expert local counsel, whose services were no longer needed.

Usually, local counsel is just hungry for billing and looking for matters that allow them to jack up their billings early. Sometimes this can be managed to the advantage of the client and ultimately, even if your firm seems to "lose" in the short term, the client will acknowledge and appreciate that you shared the reins when it was in their best interest. The strategy is thus: always keep the most important aspects of the case to yourself so that in the end you shine and keep your client for the long term. But never sacrifice the clients' interests, even if that means ceding some control to local counsel on truly local matters of utmost importance to the overall legal strategy.

## CONTINGENCY PLANNING

You'll be smart to realize that ours is now a fairly turnover-heavy profession, despite the historical track record of stability. People leave firms all the time for a variety of reasons and virtually no one is indispensable. So, as an employer, it is important to be prepared for quick change by expecting it and by thinking through as many what-ifs as you can. Contingency planning becomes incredibly valuable to help you navigate the waters with as few spills as possible. Nail down and spell out what you would do if this or that employee had to leave suddenly. Think through each of his assignments/matters in detail, what information or documents you would need to obtain from him, where they are located (hard drive, his lap top, etc.), and who would absorb the responsibilities he was currently handling. What other situations might come up and how would you deal with them? Design your organization to be flexible and create some back-up plans in case you lose a hire here and there.

The value of keeping the number of employees we had to a minimum was driven home to us only a few months into the launch of our business when we lost two employees in one week owing to personal reasons. To our surprise, we discovered that we were able to fare well for three months without rushing to hire their replacements. Since we had accrued a bit of experience in the early days managing matters ourselves, we were able to keep everything working smoothly for a while with a smaller crew. This gave us more time to find the best-fit person to replace the departed employees. We even leaned on a contractor who had some prior knowledge of our matters to get through some tough slogs. Do your best to accurately assess your work stream and hire in a way that is appropriate and fitting to it. If you get ahead of a realistic need for staff, you'll only put more pressure on yourself and the firm.

We've even taken one play out of the BigLaw playbook when it comes to hiring. When the economic crisis of 2007–2008 hit, most BigLaw firms decided to cut their mid-level associates to reduce costs. But once the economy rebounded and firms were back in the black, they didn't take any steps to replenish those positions once again. They realized that they could survive—even thrive—without mid-levels. We realized that the principle could apply to us as well so we decided not to hire mid-level associates either. We found that all of the work gets done quite well without them.

## FOCUS ON FIRM CULTURE

Frankly, we were surprised to discover how big a role our business culture plays in how effectively a candidate will fit in with the team and be effective. We learned that, at a small firm, clashes of culture and lack of "fit" are amplified and can end up causing bigger disruptions to the business in the long run. Bottom line, most people underestimate culture. We certainly did. There are many, many stories in the business media about firms underappreciating the role of healthy firm culture. So, fairly early on, even before you do any hiring, make sure you assess what your culture is, or what you are working for it to be, and evaluate how each potential candidate does or does not fit your culture. The evaluation might not be a deciding factor about a particular hire, but it can serve to get your mind in the right place to implement appropriate management procedures and it can assist you when you do your contingency planning.

Business culture comes in all sorts of shapes and sizes. Some firms are "feminine" while others are more "masculine" in tone. Some firms are very quiet and introverted while others are very loud. Some firms are fast-paced while others move rather slowly and methodically. Some law firms seem to be in hyper-growth mode while others are content to "maintain." You find some firms with more of an egalitarian ethic, and work as a unit, while others are driven by the ethos "you eat what you kill."

We are not recommending one type of culture over another and we are not writing in order to espouse the benefits of diversity, lack of diversity, or any particular type of diversity. Again, if you want the whole story on the topic of business culture, there are several books out there that do much more justice to it. But we do think that awareness of your firm's culture is very important to ensuring effective hiring and managing processes. Consider what your cultural values are and also review the things that don't jive with your culture. Maybe you missed some opportunities owing to the habits and perceptions of your culture or perhaps some things could have been done better with a slight change to your culture. It will be valuable for you to look around and take an inventory of the elements that make up your corporate culture. It will help you clarify your firm's identity and give you some parameters to discern who and what is a good fit for it.

We've found that even more important than the depth of a candidate's talent is their ability to fit in well with our culture. For example, we tend to have some aspects of a so-called "Silicon Valley" type attitude at our firm; we simply like to be comfortable and we rarely wear ties unless we're going to court. Of course, our employees can wear ties if they want to, but it's the informal, non-hierarchical, collaborative attitude that we feel enables us to work well together and get the job done. And it goes far beyond attire. For example, associates know where our firm stands in relationships with clients. They're involved in discussions about pitching to new clients, taking on new matters, and sometimes when we review payment of fees. They are present at the dinners and lunch meetings when we meet with our clients. Lots of firms' associates may see the firm's relationships with its' clients as something of a black box. There is no wall or moat keeping our staff a certain distance from the most fundamental aspects of our firm's status. This is part of our corporate culture and anyone who wants to work for us will need to feel comfortable with it.

Case in point. A few years into our firm's life, we were faced with the opportunity to hire some associates and meet the firm's growing workload. We were both working seven days a week, often to 9 or 10 p.m. at night, and were exhausted all of the time.

We were playing 'partner' and 'associate' on so many matters that we needed litigators *yesterday*. It was time to find a hire.

So we hired a highly talented litigator, whose experience consisted almost entirely of working at a law firm whose sole client was a single, large, institutional bank. He was accustomed to a very formal and rigid hierarchical work culture there and most of his experience involved dealing with middle managers who didn't have much authority or strategic expertise. His work consisted of relatively routine, small-scale litigations with similar facts, circumstances, strategy, and decisions. He wasn't used to handling major, complex matters—just the more routine ebb and flow of the same types of cases. The main goal of the middle managers with whom he worked was to avoid catastrophes and make sure that litigations filed on smoothly. He had well demonstrated his own ability to handle their cases quickly, quietly, and efficiently, so he was used to telling them what to do. Not that he couldn't handle the complex matters—those were precisely the matters for which we hired him.

In contrast to his previous employer, our firm had little formal or hierarchical structure when we hired this man. We quickly introduced him to tasks that often involved speaking directly to decision-makers and CEOs. But he wasn't used to having CEOs communicate their strategic goals and then turning around and implementing them with a well-thought-out legal strategy. In addition, while he had previously been used to a steady stream of similar matters all with the same level of risk and priority for the client, he ended up seeming to have a difficult time making the decision to adjust his work priorities between matters. We had several conversations with him in which we attempted to constructively address the mismatch between expectations and outcomes. He did end up making some very valuable contributions to certain matters, but we were never able to achieve a comfortable groove where our operation was clicking. While his background was impressive, in reality, he simply didn't fit in with our culture. We had to let him go.

It will also serve you to consider what attitudes and approaches won't work within your culture as well as what matters might be better served with a change to your culture. This self-awareness will help you hone the effectiveness of your staff as you work together. When you're hiring, you will be better equipped to ask yourself some useful questions. What situations will potential hires have to face? How are they likely to react? Is their response beneficial—or at least tolerable—to the matter, to the client and to the firm? You might decide that it is unreasonable for your culture to put an employee in a particular situation or that it might be worth it for your firm to adjust some expectations in order to accommodate an employee so that they feel that they fit with your firm. We're not talking about adopting full suit dress code or doing away with performance reviews here. We're pointing to the smaller things, like allowing for flexibility on hours, doing performance reviews a different way, changing how assignments are dispensed, and so forth. This level of flexibility can go a long way to make an employee feel comfortable.

One of our cultural values revolves around how we treat our staff. We may not be perfect at managing people, but we have discovered several ways to bring out the best in people and spot problems before they cause damage. To start, we aim to instill pride in both our employees and our interns. We introduce them to our clients; we treat them like adults; we don't treat them like indentured servants. We obviously respect the hierarchical organization and flow of command of our organization, but we don't reinforce that hierarchy with attitude. We believe that everyone deserves respect. We like to lead more than manage. It keeps everyone included, involved, and aware of what's going on. This way, we build a team of strong individuals who work well together and accomplish our firm's goals.

## MANAGING

Within our small-firm environment, after our fair share of struggles, we learned that it was perhaps easiest to look at management through the metrics of two sets of expectations—what the employees and contractors expect for their work outcomes and what we expected for the firm's project's outcomes. We found that several management issues could be attributed to discrepancies between these two sets of expectations. We now know that it is critical to our success that our expectations and our employees' expectations are communicated to each other and understood right at the outset. We believe that you can avoid many sand traps if you define, discuss, and establish your vision, goals, and expectations early in your association with those working for you. It's probably too much to hope to have perfect alignment of employee and employer expectations, but this should still be the goal that you constantly work toward in order to improve the management of your firm.

For example, an associate might think something is a low priority, but the partner needs it done well and done now to save the relationship with a client who is upset about another matter. The associate spends 12 hours on an extensive memo but the partner just needed a two-sentence email. The associate wants to move for Summary Judgment, but the client wants to get to trial as quickly as possible. The litigator who we described earlier expected to tell clients what they needed to do while we had the expectation that he would listen to clients and implement their goals into our firm's legal strategy.

When we've approached our firm to improve "management," we typically have focused on trying to achieve better alignment of firm and employee expectations for the employees' outcomes and the project outcomes. Naturally, that begins with an examination of what our expectations are and follows with an evaluation of whether those expectations are reasonable and actually align with the strategic goals we have for the firm. If we expect an employee to get something done by the end of the day, that expectation should be borne by a desired project outcome, namely the satisfactory completion of the work matter to the benefit of the client. We don't want to expect an assignment to be done by the end of the day when in truth we think that employee has been slacking and we want to punish him or crack him into shape. It doesn't work out that way. Not only would this approach not make sense to our overall goals for the assignment, it's a poor way to convince the employee not to slack off. It's especially true if he gets an idea that we set deadlines arbitrarily or at least not in accord with the overall project goals.

Here are some ways you can improve the alignment of your firm's expectations with those of your employees. First, focus on clear and consistent communication of expectations on both sides. You can delineate your expectations for job roles, goals, behavior, and outcomes of specific matters, for example. When things about the assignment change, make sure you clearly communicate to the team that your expectations about the project have changed. Convey what you expect in the way of workflow and project outcomes, how you reward stellar work with bonuses, and how raises are usually tied to meeting specific goals that the firm has for them.

You might set milestones for progress and completion on particular matters, which allow more fluidity than billed hours. You can set expectations for producing a certain level of draft in a certain amount of time. You can say that you want A, B, and C done by the end of the month, and if it doesn't happen, then in the next performance review, you review and address why not. And it goes without saying that memorializing your meetings and the expectations you discussed is essential. Several of these tactics involve follow through so make sure you actually match the follow through with the stated expectations and outcomes. In our experience, our employees respond rationally to what is communicated to them and if our follow through doesn't match what we stated from the outset, they learn to second guess what we said and try to decipher our expectations despite our communication. This is a waste of resources and causes friction between us and our employees. We like to believe that employees are spending most if not all of their time working on projects and figuring out ways to get the job done better and faster. But if we are honest with ourselves, they are often thinking about what we say, what we want, and how we are likely to react to situations. The more we can take the guesswork out of the process, the less time employees will spend thinking about the things that are not directly productive for the firm.

Once an associate has been with your firm for a few months, you begin to expect him or her to be able to handle certain decisions or take on actions on his own. He should be able to field a preliminary call with a client, for example, describing his problem or what he needed, and then bring it up for discussion internally and formulate a plan of action for client approval. If he has not met these development expectations, why not? It's likely that you have not incentivized him effectively. Maybe he wasn't aware of your expectation; maybe it wasn't expressed clearly enough; or maybe you hadn't fully conveyed its level of priority to your firm. You might want to communicate that there will be consequences to failing to meet those kinds of expectations. You should give him feedback and guidance about whether he's doing a good job or not and foster his ability to handle those calls on his own.

Somewhat surprisingly, the most common complaint we hear about working for any sized firm is about associates feeling undue pressure to bring in clients on their own. So we made a commitment to ourselves that we would never rely on our associates for business development. We have no expectations or demand that they bring clients in the door for us, and we communicate that explicitly. However, given the close nature of our client relationships and the transparency of our interactions, they'll end up learning a lot about client development as they spend time with our firm, and they can contribute in that way down the line if they choose to.

Regular performance reviews are a must. For any firm that's hell-bent on being an expert in their niche—like us—it's absolutely critical to set up performance reviews with each employee to discuss his work and the firm's expectations for his engagement in the future. These regularly scheduled meetings help you get on the same page with your employee, set new goals and expectations, and spot any early warning signs of degradation of performance or attitude. Review whether or not the employee met your expectations. If not, what did he fall short on? Was it something that was mission-critical or was it something that you had not addressed or anticipated with him? It's a time to seek correction to any unsatisfactory work and to improve behaviors that will have a positive result. Communication is key. You need to communicate your expectations and confirm that each employee understands those expectations. It is a good time to determine if that employee is progressing satisfactorily in growing his knowledge of your niche. It's also helpful for your employee to communicate his expectations and for you to confirm that you understand those as well. You can implement those expectations through plans of action and by the judicious use of deadlines. Of course, deadlines can be fluid, especially in a small firm where matters can expand and contract unceremoniously and firm resources are more flexible.

The expectations you address can pertain to employee behaviors or can focus on the outcomes of certain matters. You might set benchmarks of progress, like what items are completed by the end of the month for example, instead of hard-billed hours. If those goals aren't achieved, then the subsequent performance review should address why not.

Performance reviews are also great opportunities for you as the manager/principal to get new perspectives on the firm's matters and the firm itself. Heck, you might even learn about your own management performance as well.

## INCENTIVES

Knowing what motivates each of your staff can play a huge role in understanding their expectations and in turn motivating them to perform in ways that achieve the results that you expect. When you have a clear understanding of their motivations, you can use that knowledge to align them with the goals and expectations of your firm. As a result, you'll create a more productive workforce, generate more loyalty, and increase employee satisfaction, which of course, prompts them to work harder for you.

We've learned you can start as early as the first interview to discover what fuels an individual's desire to work at all, and work for you in particular. Ask directly to get a general sense of what is motivating him or her. What is inspiring him to take a job with your firm? What's behind her efforts to seek a job at all? What gets them out of bed on any particular morning? How does this job fit with their overall life goals? And beyond that: what will keep him working on a Friday afternoon when the partners are at the beach and the staff has taken an early afternoon? Answers to these questions will give you valuable data about how to manage them, how productive they can be, and whether or not they can align with your firm's goals and expectations.

When it comes to incentives, we might assume that the usual list of salary, bonus, health insurance, and vacations are all that matter to the people we hire. But times have changed since the material things were of greatest concern; intangibles can have just as much perceived value than tangible benefits, if not more so. We just looked at ourselves and our motivations of leaving our BigLaw jobs to understand that there are more motivators than a steady, relatively high paycheck and/or BigLaw prestige. Concerns like reputation, autonomy, experience, lifestyle, and reduced stress can play a large role in motivating your employees, keeping them focused, and creating job satisfaction.

Stress comes up a lot in our discussions with job candidates, too. We've interviewed and hired many who told us they were more than willing to take a reduction in salary in exchange for a

reduction in the amount of stress they experience on the job. For
some, it meant being able to plug away on motions and not have to
deal with client calls and lunches all of the time. For others, it
meant being able to leave at 5 p.m. to pick up their daughter from
school. Still others didn't want to have to dread being asked to pull
all-nighters once a month.

For very experienced lawyers, there is an advantage that fewer
hours can be traded for a salary discount. The same goes for your
new hires. You can get them on a monetary discount compared with
the larger law firms competing for their talent. The cherry on top is
that you're offering much more interesting work in a complex and
substantive area of law that's more stimulating to them beyond the
"consumer law" or personal injury law firms popular in every
American city. You offer prestige, since they will learn expertise in
your special business niche. You also offer hands-on experience that
can be valuable to a big firm and to an in-house law department.

By the way, one of the most counterintuitive discoveries we've
made is what we call the "firm phone factor." You should be aware
that a firm-provided mobile phone carries a lot more weight than its
4 or 5 ounces. We found it to be a pretty uniform phenomenon:
employees put a high value on having their mobile phone paid for
by the firm. When speaking to family members or other attorney
friends, associates very much want to be able to say that their firm
pays for their phone. It has an outsized impact on their perception
of your firm. Of course, to you, it is a minor expense when
compared with the rest of the firm's overhead; and indeed the
marginal cost is reduced even further as you add more employees.
These small comfort items, like paying for a coffee machine and
taking employees out to lunch regularly, are small-ticket items that
have a big impact on motivation. Take it from us, there is something
to be said (by your hires) for a firm that pays for their cell phone.

## BONUSES

And then there are bonuses. Bonuses reinforce loyalty and effort,
especially when you've done your homework about where an
employee's values and incentives lie. Hours-based bonuses make
sense for large firms, but they don't necessarily always make sense
for smaller law firms. For a small firm like ours, giving bonuses

based on successes goes a long way to emphasize the firm's expectations and incentivizes employees. When you award a bonus owing to a breakthrough or big win for the firm, you align the employee's incentives with those of the firm. The employee recognizes the interdependence of his individual rewards with the success of the firm, and your goals become his goals, too. However, it's important to recognize that firm successes are not always driven primarily through the contributions of the firm's team. Sometimes luck plays a role, and rewarding a bonus based on luck doesn't necessarily enhance an employee's belief that their work in promoting the firm's interests is the surest way to be rewarded financially. Similarly, bad luck does not necessarily mean that heads must roll. Reductions in bonus or reprimand should not be meted out just because something bad happened. Only when poor performance is clearly the direct cause of the undesirable outcome does it make sense to tie negative performance to a reduced bonus.

You might reward an employee with a bonus for her extra effort in a particularly important matter. Or, you can do it the other way around: if a key client has a significant matter that you absolutely need to get done right, you can offer a bonus ahead of time to those employees who successfully produce the result you're looking for.

You can also consider offering shared revenue from a particular client or matter as a variant on a bonus. If an associate was instrumental in bringing the client to your firm, go ahead and offer a bonus. Again, you'll be fueling her incentives and aligning them with your expectations.

When it comes to calculating bonuses, keep in mind that since the work we do in a small law firm is so fluid and variable, it makes the most sense to offer individualized bonuses that are calculated on a case-by-case basis. Set them according to the work accomplished and, in some cases, the financial arrangements of the matter. Offering only one standard bonus doesn't make sense for your small law firm since some clients get charged more than others.

The same can be said for raises. While BigLaw employees are stuck in a rigid raise structure, your small firm can create more flexible rules for raises based on whether an employee has met or exceeded your expectations.

Interestingly, we discovered that when bonuses are given unexpectedly, the gesture has a much greater impact on increasing employee satisfaction than those that are expected or routine. Calculating and implementing bonuses and pay raises in this somewhat bespoke manner does require more time and effort on the part of firm management. It is more difficult to substantively review performance, outcomes, and progress than it is to give a bonus check every year and simply verify hours. But the extra work pays off by improving the alignment between your incentives and expectations. It reinforces expectations and provides maximum motivation geared toward generating beneficial firm outcomes.

While as a firm we want to maximize our output and have our employees be as productive as reasonably possible, we also want to maintain a very human environment. To us, that means we simply have to track hours. But we don't micro-manage people. We don't review billable hours religiously, enforce a minimum billable hour requirement, or tie bonuses to billable hours. We focus on the matters at hand.

In this chapter, we've taken a dive into the management principles by which we operate, namely, that to effectively manage a firm, you must focus on aligning employee expectations of their outcomes with your firm's expectations for project outcomes. We explained that in order to align expectations, it's helpful to begin with thoughtful internal evaluation, and proceed to consistent communication, with a focus on employee motivations. We then illustrated how these processes can be implemented with tangible policies such as performance reviews and performance-based compensation. In the next chapter, we'll examine a critical decision in the process of starting a business niche law firm: whether or not, and with whom one should begin a partnership.

# 7.  Is partnership right for me?

When you're considering launching your own law firm, one of the first questions you'll want to answer for yourself is whether or not you want to go solo or whether you want to take on a partner or partners. After all, starting, managing, and successfully sustaining a new law business is a complex undertaking. Initially, it may seem like an easy and obvious choice to make but we encourage you to resist the temptation to approach such a decision with complacency. It just might be the most important (and most difficult to unwind) decision you make for your law firm.

Whomever you choose to be at the helm of your firm – whether it's you alone or a partnership of several – will chart the direction, establish the tone, and make decisions that will decide the success of your business for years to come.

In this chapter, we'll first take a quick look at when it might be a good choice for you to be a solo attorney. (Spoiler alert: very rarely.) Then we'll walk you through what to look for if you've decided to establish a partnership. We'll give you a heads up about the three critical elements that will make a successful, long-term law partnership successful. If you're thinking of establishing a partnership with more than two partners, we won't bc addressing issues pertaining to partnerships of that size simply because we don't have any personal experience with it. You'll have other considerations to take into account that we won't cover here. However, this chapter will be a good place for you to start to learn about some of the critical issues of any business partnership.

## GOING SOLO

Launching and running a law firm is a rapid, complex, and ever-evolving series of responsibilities and decisions. It's a lot for two people to handle, let alone just one. If you're thinking of going solo, an important question to ask yourself is: how long you can sustain an intense pace of competing demands, fulfilling long- and short-term goals, and a wide variety of low- and high-level tasks? Think about it. There's setting business objectives, goals, and policies; hiring, firing, and managing staff; formulating and carrying out strategies for each matter you have before you; thinking through how each matter affects the overall strategy of your firm; managing cash flow and expenses; having a strong grasp of ethics; avoiding high risk; knowing when to take risks; setting and keeping deadlines; legal research; drafting legal briefs; going to court, talking to judges, litigating; answering and returning phone calls and emails; setting rates; bookkeeping, bill collecting and having difficult conversations with clients about late payments; pitching, closing, and wining and dining clients; effectively solving problems that arise every day. Etc., etc., etc. You'll need to do all of these things, all of the time, every day, for the rest of your law firm's life.

If we are being brutally honest, we would admit that most people cannot do this. Most lawyers cannot do this. Surely lots of lawyers already trying to do this may find they cannot sustain. There may actually be a few people out there who can manage the entire scope of the business all on their own, and create a suitable lifestyle as they do so, but as you've probably guessed, we don't recommend trying it as a one-person operation. If you're exceptionally brilliant at a lot of things, if you're much more comfortable working alone than with others, and if you're okay with having the burden of every aspect of the business on your shoulders, it might be worth considering. And it's not good enough to just be good at these things – you must be *very* good at all of these things to make your solo firm sustainable. In a partnership, you can get away with being only okay, or even not so good, at some of these things, but going solo without being very good at everything can threaten the sustainability of your firm over the long run.

If you don't think you can trust anyone else with the secrets of your business and you strongly desire to control most aspects of your life, then you might not have a choice in the matter. You may not be able to find a partner to tolerate you. If you are leaning in that direction, we just highly recommend that you be honest with yourself. Anyone can run a law firm really well for a few days. Anybody can maintain a good relationship with a client over a number of years. But can you do those and many other things, really well, every day for a number of years? And do you really want to risk your business reputation and financial security on that question? Again, this is a matter of achieving sustainability – a concept we've already mentioned several times, and to which we will devote a chapter of its own. For now, we will focus exclusively on how partnering fits into the quest for sustainability because it's that important to your law firm.

## PICKING THE RIGHT PARTNER

Many of us may want a business partner to start a new business venture because we honestly admit that we can't do everything ourselves all of the time. You may have undertaken a rigorously honest assessment of your skills and temperament and wisely inferred that you lack a skill, ability, or attribute to build a sustainable solo practice. On the other hand, you may also prefer a partnership in order to increase your chances of succeeding in growing a law firm, and attain all that comes with it, in the manner that you desire. After all, two heads and two sets of hands are often better than one. In a partnership, you won't have to singlehandedly master the entire range of talents and skills that your firm will require of you. Your team of two can much more readily and more effectively take care of the full range of responsibilities necessary to build your practice, your reputation, and your profits, than you could do alone.

So if you decide to form a partnership, you should start by recognizing something that is probably obvious but worth stating: that the quality of your relationship with your partner needs to be excellent. You're about to embark on a long-term relationship, after all, and you'll be placing the health of your business and its future and of your life in their hands as much as your own. You could say that picking a business partner is similar to picking a marriage partner in that you'll be spending a lot of time together (most of your waking hours, for sure) and building a future together. You want to be happy with them all along the way and will need the relationship to grow for your firm to be sustainable.

So how do you evaluate who might be a good partner for you? We found that there are three characteristics that must be present in a business partnership for it to have any hope of surviving and thriving, namely, unconditional trust, a complementary set of talents and skills, and an alignment of motivating factors that drive you to succeed.

## TRUST

Simply put, your relationship with your partner has to begin with trust. Whether you've known each other for a long time or you've asked enough questions and engaged in enough relationship-building to feel fully satisfied and comfortable with your new partner, you have to establish a strong sense of confidence and trust in the other. They should not be someone you met on Craigslist and had coffee with a few times. After all, life is full of challenges and situations that arise that ask a lot of us. During those times, you'll want your partner to show up with as much proficiency and good judgment as you would. If you don't trust your partner, then you will be much more vulnerable to undesirable outcomes when challenging times arise. The ultimate test is: can you swap your partner for yourself in any business situation? Think about the tasks that you need to take that day, that week, or for a given assignment. If you don't feel 100% confident with having your partner take that off your hands, it's time to look for a new partner.

Part of the reason our own partnership works so well is that we had been friends for five years before we initiated our business partnership. We met each other during the first week of law school and grew our relationship from there. We lived in the same apartment together. We studied for the bar exam together – a challenging experience that tested both of us and allowed us to see how each operates and solves problems under pressure. We even traveled through Europe together. All of these experiences grew the trust we had with each other as well as giving us an inside look at what was motivating each of us in different situations.

A good partner will be someone whom you can trust with every detail of your business finances and legal standings, and whom you'd have no hesitation giving full access to any document within the company. You want to trust their ability to respond to any task or respond to situations with the same level of integrity and efficacy as you would. You want to feel very comfortable with putting things in their hands. That won't necessarily mean that you are both equally good at doing everything. We were not. No two people will be. Everybody's got their unique set of strengths and weaknesses. But you need to honestly feel confident in handing over any task for your partner to do. We had come to know each other so well and operated on such a high level of trust that we knew virtually everything about each other's finances and personal lives. We were open books to each other. That's the level of trust you need to make a partnership work.

We mention that we shared accounts and finances to underscore the amount of trust we had for each other before we launched a business together. But we must also point out that this trust was correlated with a rigorous honesty between each other. We trusted each other enough to be open and honest about everything, from professional to anything personal, which would potentially impact the partnership. At the same time, we actively worked on getting out our feelings on any and all of these situations, so that we both expected rigorous honesty. We could proceed knowing that we had full and accurate information about the other partner's thoughts or feelings on a given subject. This level of trust, and rigorous honesty, was critical in allowing us to deftly handle difficult situations that inevitably arise in the running of a law firm.

You also want to feel good about their grasp of ethics and find out where they stand on ethical issues. As we'll discuss in the next chapter, ethical considerations should be part of the fabric of your ongoing business discussions. But you're not going to be able to sit down with your partner and drill down into every single ethical decision that has to be made for the partnership. You want to feel that when they need to make a judgment call on their own, they're going to make the best call for you and for the partnership. You want to feel that you both share similar values and objectives.

How do you determine if you can trust someone you're considering partnering with? If you've known that person for a while, then you've had the requisite time to build trust with him or her. If you don't know your potential partner very well, then be willing to take the time to get to know them and see if you can develop a sure sense of trust. Recognize that it's not something that you can rush; it will happen at its own pace. In fact, if you try too hard to move too quickly, you could short circuit the process to your detriment.

So be willing to take some time to develop your relationship and to find out if you feel you can trust the other person implicitly. Get together and discuss things like the direction, goals, strategies, and objectives of the firm you'd like to start. Talk about decision-making itself and flesh out how you both see that happening. Be honest with yourself, too. If something feels off about the person, trust that. Don't override your inner sense of them. If appropriate, address your concern by talking about it with them. That feeling is probably telling you something helpful.

Trust will be a cornerstone of your partnership relationship and needs to be maintained over the long haul. Once you're in business together, if one of you does something that undermines some of the trust you've built for each other, you'll need to address the issue right away and try to fix it. You can't set it aside and you can't ignore it because it will damage the very foundation of your business. And honestly, if you can't fix it, then you will probably end up having to abandon the partnership. That's how important trust is to your business.

## COMPLEMENTARY SKILLS

In a perfect world, you and your partner would both be masters of all the skills that a law firm requires to be successful. You could pick and choose who's going to do what at any point in time based solely on availability or choice. From litigation to sales to answering phone calls and dealing with billing – and every other one of the myriad skills that are required – either one of you could handle things professionally, proficiently, successfully, and on a moment's notice.

When the two of us started talking about forming a business partnership, we realized that we had highly complementary sets of skills. That meant that we could each spend the bulk of our time doing what we enjoy and do best – and trust the other to do the same. Our personalities and strengths are different enough that we can dive into our work with a high level of expertise and success and leave the other to do the same in their work. Yussuf is great at exploring marketing strategies, meeting with clients, and building the business, for example, while Jacob can spend hours researching issues and analyzing cases. It's not that we can't do what the other does – we can and do; it's just that it's a smarter use of time if we assign to each other what we each do best. We don't have to duplicate efforts. We're able to leverage what we're good at.

But it's not a perfect world, so you need to aim to be able to cover all of the many roles and responsibilities of your firm between the two of you. If it were a puzzle with each piece representing a role or responsibility to run a law firm, and if you had all the pieces within your own reach, you might be one of the rare birds who could consider running your firm solo. But for the rest of us, some of the pieces to the puzzle are missing, or maybe half-formed. At the same time, for your new law firm to succeed, you need to have all of the pieces present and fitting in the right places. The beauty of partnership is it allows you to work with someone whose skills and talents complement your own, fill in for what you lack, and vice versa.

For the same reasons, if you are considering partnering with someone who has the exact same puzzle pieces as you have, and is missing the same ones too, you won't have what it takes to run your company. In that case, you need to either find a different partner or find a third partner to fill in the gaps.

But realistically, if you're going to be a small, independent, nimble, successful firm focusing on a niche market – whether you're a solo venture or a partnership – you have to at least be comfortable doing everything. On any given day, you may find yourself in situations where you have to be able to handle anything that comes up, and do it well. But that doesn't mean you *always* have to handle everything.

While Jacob had no love for going to court or arguing motions before a judge, he didn't set a policy that he would never go to court. That wouldn't be feasible. He's done it several times, gets the job done, and over time, he has become more and more successful with it. Of course, no one is going to mistake him for F. Lee Bailey, but he can go into a courtroom and present an argument effectively. But when Yussuf is available, we both prefer that he be the one to do so.

We don't mean to suggest that this is an exact science. You don't have to write a list or divvy up responsibilities one by one to cover every base. But it's a good thing to consider as you get to know someone and consider them for your business partnership. You'll pick up clues and learn what they have and haven't done, and what roles they have and haven't taken. Are you two exactly alike or are your skills and experiences complementary? Is there a piece missing? It's a good thing to keep an eye out for. And if there is a piece missing, figure out what you're going to do about it.

Discovering which talents and skills the two of you share and which ones you don't is a process as much as developing trust in your partner is a process. It takes time to unfold and gel, so let it happen. Don't throw in the towel just because one person isn't good at something. Don't be afraid to readjust roles and tasks in response to their relative strengths and weaknesses after they've put effort into certain tasks. But do look for a set of talents and skills in your partner that are sufficiently different from yours to serve the business well.

## MOTIVATIONAL ALIGNMENT

Along with unconditional trust and complementary skills, the third essential element for a partnership to succeed is having a virtually identical alignment of motivations. Everybody has their unique incentives and motivating drives that propel them to pursue law and to open a practice or, simply put, to wake up and go to work in the morning. We believe that one of the things that helped our firm be as successful as it is, is that the two of us have a tremendous commonality in what motivates us. We could safely say that what drives both of us is at least 90% identical. Realistically, your incentives and driving ambitions should mirror each other at least to a sufficient degree for you to work well together and build a law practice that grows and grows. Too many differences can cause friction and disagreement in objectives and operations that can be very difficult to get past. The more alike you are, the easier it will be for you to move forward harmoniously and swiftly.

So what are the motivational factors? For those of us who have the drive and determination to go to law school, pass the bar, and seek a career in law, there are usually up to four motivating factors involved: money, prestige, self-fulfillment, and outside interests. For most of us, the vision of making a lot of money has played a big role in why we pursue a career in law. It's what energizes us, gets us up in the morning, and it makes those long hours all worth it. Second, some of us are also motivated by a drive for prestige – a feeling of being important in your own eyes and in the eyes of others. You just have to have the large office, the orchids in the lobby, the impressive original artwork, and your name on the door.

Third, some seek self-fulfillment through their career. They want to feel that they're making a contribution to the world by representing those in need, representing those who have been wronged, or doing work that advances the well-being of humankind. Finally, there are those who are driven by other interests, like those who simply find the law intellectually challenging, those who work primarily because they care to create meaningful relationships with others, or those who simply want to work to earn just enough to get by so that they can spend most of their other time doing some other activity, like painting, collecting, or live action role plays.

Everybody's unique combination of their goals, intentions, and priorities – their *motivational hierarchy* – drives them toward their goals. These are what determine the choices you make, the strategies you like, and the direction you set for your organization. They impact who you hire, how you organize your firm, the goals you set, and the strategies you implement to reach success as you define it. If your motivations are very different, then many of the preferences and strategies you'll want to make for your business will also differ greatly and that will be difficult to navigate through the years. That's why it's so important that you and your partner have a high degree of alignment in what is motivating you.

Motivational alignment might not be so obvious, so don't make snap judgments before you ask a lot of questions. Let's say a 28-year-old lawyer and a 45-year-old lawyer with a wife and kids meet to talk about launching a law firm, for example. On the surface, it might seem as though their lifestyles could easily appear to be too different to be able to forge a long-term, successful partnership. On the other hand, if they are sufficiently similar in their pursuit of profit and profit alone, then the other considerations might not matter. Maybe the 45-year-old ignores his kids. Maybe the 28-year-old ignores calls from his friends to go to clubs on weekends and eschews the other benefits of a single life. If they're sufficiently motivated by the same things, then they could potentially succeed together.

On the other hand, two people might have a similar drive to make a lot of money, for example, but if you dig deeper, you might find subtle differences in what they're seeking and why. One person might aim to make enough money to sustain his comfortable lifestyle and cover his expenses while the next guy or gal is driven to make as much money as humanly possible. You can imagine that if they were considering forming a partnership, they could easily run into differences that could cause problems for the smooth operation of the partnership. They may be in for a lot of confrontations and contention as the years roll on.

We clearly had very similar motivations when we considered joining efforts to form a partnership. We both had begun our careers in BigLaw but had become dissatisfied with all that entailed and sought more control over our work and career. We each came from humble means and graduated with significant student loan burdens, so earning money to clear those obligations quickly was very important to both of us. Finally, we were both in our late 20s, single, and enjoyed having some time to work on fitness and fun. We liked exercising at the gym and playing pickup basketball, but we also enjoyed going out to socialize, meet friends, and make new friends in a large city. It was a natural match of motivations. Any differences might have hindered efforts to get the firm off the ground, for example, if one of us didn't have a lot of student debt or if one of us had started a family and had kids. Overall our motivations were aligned nearly all of the time. In other words, our business strategy for the firm was nearly always in harmony with our reasons for being in the partnership.

It's also revealing to ask yourself how you and your potential partner's motivations might change over the course of time. Will you still be compatible enough? How much will the motivations of the 28-year-old and 45-year-old above change over time? In five years, when the older partner's kids are having kids of their own, will he still be willing to turn his back on family life? Will he want to retire? What if the 28-year-old falls in love? Will his motivations change?

Indeed, the very success of the law firm you build can change your motivational drives. If your firm does well for itself in your niche and makes a lot of money for you and your partner, then either one of you might end up feeling that making money has become less of a priority. And that can change everything.

## MOTIVATIONS CAN CHANGE

Once you begin running your business with your partner, you'll inevitably come across some differences of opinion and preferences as you decide strategies, organize operations, and grow your business. As your company grows, you'll want to keep an eye on these discrepancies of direction. No two people are exactly alike so differences can be expected. But if it becomes the norm, it can signal that there's a deeper problem – a divergence in motivation.

Maybe your motivations are very much the same in the beginning, but then they get more divergent more regularly. For example, if you start to notice that one of you wants to keep the amount of time and effort devoted to developing new business the same, while the other wants to push forward and open up a whole new niche, it could be symptoms of a divergence of underlying motivations. If, after you've reached a certain level of success, one of you loses their motivation for money and simply wants to maintain the status quo for your business development, while the other partner, highly motivated by money, wants to take excessive amounts of risk to grow the business, it could be a game changer. If you are too different, someone is going to start getting unhappy and fast.

Being aware of the differences in what motivates you and being honest with yourselves about them can help smooth over the smaller problems and re-align you both with the greater objective of running a successful firm. If you are well aware of the ways in which your motivations are dissimilar, you can factor that in as you have your debates and discussions about your firm's goals and strategic objectives. You can sit down and discuss some sort of middle ground that doesn't throw the law firm completely off course or cause an irreparable schism in the direction of the firm. But if your motivations are dramatically different, there will come a point at which it's no longer sustainable or advantageous to maintain a partnership. It will happen if the motivations are sufficiently divergent.

Some people make the mistake of having an ulterior motive when they decide to launch a new practice and build a business of law. The problem with going ahead with such an effort that way is that those hidden motivations will ultimately win out in the end – and will likely sabotage the business.

For example, some lawyers have no love for law and probably shouldn't have gone to law school. Some of them favor business over law, and think that if they start a firm, they can spend their time running the business instead of practicing law. But that would be a huge mistake. It would be better to find a business that you don't dislike so much and do that. Even if you've sunk your savings into the cost of a law degree, you'd be better served by getting out of the law. The passion you have for the work you do carries you through the challenging times. If you don't honestly have an interest in the law or get some satisfaction from reading an interesting case or learning how things shake out from a legal perspective, then you'll probably flame out quickly.

It also pays to stay aware of your own motivations as you run your firm. Not only can your motivations change over time, but sometimes they can surprise you. You could be in a meeting and agree wholeheartedly with your partner on a certain strategic direction, for example. But later, when you are carrying out that decision, maybe you feel conflict with that decision. That could be the signal that some hidden motivation is clashing with what you've agreed to. Do some internal inventory and clarify where your motivations lie. Then you'll understand more about what you're seeking, and you'll be better prepared to go after that, or negotiate, or do what it takes to find the right solutions.

## "INTERVIEWING" A PROSPECTIVE PARTNER

When you're seeking a partner for your law firm, you'll want to interview your prospective partner as much as you'd interview a new hire – or more. To be clear, we are not advocating that you begin a partnership with a stranger. This is but one element of a long-term process of getting to know another person for the purposes of evaluating a possibility of partnership. These questions should be addressed at some point – even if you've known the other person for 5+ years – just as we knew each other for that long before deciding to partner with each other. Here are some very helpful questions for you both to ask yourselves:

- Where do you see yourself in 5 years?
- What are your goals for 10 years from now?

- Why do you want to start a law firm? What's motivating you?
- Why do you want to start *this* law firm?
- If you don't do this now, what's your fall back? (This question helps to glean motivations.)
- Do you think that the law firm is highly likely to deliver on what you're hoping to get from it?
- What do you think will be motivating you in 5, 10, or 15 years into the future?
- What do you do when you're not practicing law?
- Why did you go into law?
- What assignments do you like most? Least?
- Why do you think you will be good at running a law firm?
- Why would you prefer to partner up instead of going solo?

Of course, these questions are just the start of many long conversations that will help you decide if someone is the right person for you to form a partnership with or not. Pay attention to whether or not you feel an implicit sense of trust in them that you can initiate a long and fruitful partnership. Compare and contrast skills and talents to see if you complement each other well enough to be able to accomplish the huge task of launching a successful law firm. And discuss and discover what precisely is motivating each of you and whether those factors are at least 90% in alignment. Take the time to do all this with care; it will be worth it.

Building a thriving small law firm from scratch is a large, intense undertaking and will most likely require a partnership of some kind to share the duties, the decision-making, the vision, the stress, and the success. That understood, it then behooves you to take the time and put in the effort to explore partnership candidates effectively, so that you choose one with the best combination of skills, personality, motivations, and temperament to see you through to long-term success. Finding someone whom you can trust unconditionally with every aspect of the business and who has a highly complementary skill set to your own will allow you to focus on the most important thing: delivering great services to your clients. Finally, ensuring that your and your partner's motivations are highly aligned will help you sidestep inevitable misunderstandings and divergence of direction that could sabotage all of your best efforts.

In the next chapter, we'll talk about ethics. No, it's not a throw-away chapter. For a business-niche-driven, small law firm like yours, there is great benefit and strategic power to making the small sacrifices it takes to hew to ethical guidelines. We'll share with you how to include ethical considerations into many of your firm's activities and gain the significant advantage from doing so.

# 8.  An argument for ethics

We know what you're thinking as you read the title of this chapter.

You're thinking that this chapter's only here because our publisher wouldn't let us release our book if it was too short – so we thought we'd throw in a chapter on "ethics" as a filler. Or maybe you think we included it to help our book get on the shelves of law schools and bar association libraries. Well, your assumptions are correct in one way: ethics isn't the sexiest topic in the world. But we don't include this chapter out of some base ulterior motive. We do so because we want your small business-niche-based law firm to gain respect, traction, and profitability as quickly as possible. And that includes clear and substantive considerations of ethics.

Now, most law schools barely appear to give the topic of ethics any priority; they don't even pretend to provide any kind of in-depth *practical* examination of ethics – its complexities, the long-term impact of your ethical choices, and how to discern what side of the line to choose under what conditions. In law school, maybe a few hours of a few sessions of your 1L course seminar will be devoted to "Ethics." And if you're like most other students in your class, you'll sit there, bored, pecking at your laptop, not really paying attention. Not until your third year of law school will you revisit the topic when it comes time to take the Multistate Professional Responsibility Examination (MPRE). A 60-question, 120-minute, national pass/fail test, the MPRE is designed to measure your understanding of proper professional conduct for attorneys. But studying for it will demand relatively little time and will provide little insight into how to contend with actual, real-life, real-time, ethical questions at your own law firm.

At best, the education that law schools provide about ethics is a minimal, theoretical perspective and a perfunctory exercise to encourage you to do the "right" thing. Beyond that, it's not much help. It doesn't look into real-world practical examples of how appropriate ethics can be implemented or provide meaningful guidance to help you make wise ethical choices. There's an immense difference between answering a conflict of interest, multiple-choice question on the MPRE and knowing how to deal with a potential dispute between two of your clients who are getting involved in business pursuits. This is a failure of legal education – but we won't belabor this sad state of affairs. We'll defer to the countless legal journalists and Twitter commentators as to how to remedy this situation. In this book, we're only concerned about what this means for us as we are trying to build a successful, independent, legal practice.

Fast-forward a few years into your practice and, after researching a thorny and uncertain regulatory issue, your client's general counsel disagrees with your analysis. He says that, despite your findings that a certain practice may be prohibited, he interprets the lack of definiteness under the law as permission, and will continue to counsel his client to engage in the conduct in question.

What will you do at that point? And how likely is it that you'll resort to thinking about what the MPRE practice questions said about such a situation?

This chapter takes a practical, inside look at ethics from the perspective of a small law firm specializing in a particular business niche. While adopting and following ethical guidelines will benefit any lawyer or businessperson, doing so can also be an especially valuable business-development tactic if you are launching a new small firm. On the other hand, it may appear to present short-term challenges or cause you to lose out on some short-term gains.

## ETHICS AS A TACTIC

Many people and most lawyers assume that there's some sort of sacrifice that comes with walking the straight and narrow path of ethics. But our experience tells us this is often an inflated perception; it only seems that way because you may be pitting short-term costs against long-term gains. While looking after your ethical welfare can present short-term sacrifices from time to time, they will typically provide long-term benefits to your practice and your firm. Ultimately, doing so helps you gain new clients, manage your firm more effectively, and make decisions about challenging matters that will help to extend the longevity and reach of your law firm business. Responding to an ethical compass is another tactic you implement to quickly and sustainably succeed as a new, small law firm. As we will come full circle to in the next chapter, ethics is a huge driver of firm sustainability.

While being mindful of ethical considerations is advisable (and obligatory) for all lawyers, it is especially worthwhile if you've adopted a business-niche specialization strategy for your firm. Operating within a business niche means that you will be circulating in overlapping circles; you will have clients that are friends, clients that are competitors, clients that are sworn arch-nemeses, vendors and customers. You are not operating in a vast vacuum. Because of that, you'll be interacting with a smaller number of players than you would otherwise. That environment can become something of a fishbowl: successes, failures, and incidents of any kind will be broadcast throughout the community of your niche. Any brushes with ethics will become much more visible to other lawyers and to your potential clients within your industry. A scandal in a large city is going to get less notoriety than one in a tiny town where everybody knows your name. A potential client can hear nice things about you from others on ten different occasions, but if one person tells them that you're unethical, you can safely assume they won't accept your pitch for new representation.

Regardless of whether you are niche-specialized or you're a general services attorney, the risks of participating in less-than-ethical activity can be extremely costly. From loss of reputation, professional responsibility board action, governmental investigations, lawsuits and worse, the downside of not thinking through the ethical ramifications of your actions and your firm's actions can be devastating. You need to take ethics seriously.

Especially when it comes to law, ethical issues can arise at any time in the course of working for a client or attending to specific matters. In other words, you should expect them to occur – because they will, often when you don't expect them. That's why we strongly recommend that you take on a proactive approach to ethics. Always be on the lookout for what could be ethically problematic in the long run. Build in ethics decision points at each major juncture of your practice to make sure that you consider potential ethical considerations in virtually all of your firm's activities. For example, when you decide to take on a new client, consider the ethics implications. When you're publishing a new article, take time to ask yourselves what ethical implications might be involved. When you're taking on a new matter for an existing client, think through what might be the potential ethics implications of the matter. Like mapping out a decision tree, forecast the potential outcomes, twists, and turns of each lawsuit and then consider what might be the potential ethical implications of each one of those twists and turns.

Let's say a client comes to you and tells you he is desperate for a legal opinion backing up the legality of his next proposed business transaction. You have some familiarity with the type of arrangement and with the relevant authorities, although you will have to do some more research and render your legal analysis. Based on your familiarity with the issue, you already have some serious doubts about the legality of the arrangement. There is some gray area, but the arrangement clearly does not meet the spirit of a safe harbor regulation, even if it might not technically violate any explicit prohibition. You will write the opinion letter, but you want to make clear that your client may not like the content.

Now what if we told you that this client owed you several months' worth of legal fees? Would that change how eager you would be to find a way to write the opinion that the client wants? You may look a little harder at the existing legal authorities and secondary sources. It is only natural: psychologists call this common type of behavior *loss aversion*. Ironically, people are typically *risk averse* when it comes to going after gains. We'll take the sure $100 rather than risk flipping a coin for either $300 or nothing. Yet when we are facing losses, we actually seek risk in order to avoid the loss, especially if it is a financial loss. If a lawyer faced our hypothetical situation, his loss aversion human behavioral heuristic would tempt him to write the opinion favorably in order to forestall any risk of losing what he was owed in legal fees.

Situations like this are good reminders that we all need to be reminded to comply with ethical obligations at all times. A proactive approach to ethics would require each assignment to undergo an ethical analysis prior to beginning, at which point the good lawyer may acknowledge his desire to avoid ruffling the feathers of the erstwhile client. We are no behavioral psychologists, but our strategy for combatting these (realistic and probable) scenarios is through proactively making ethical analysis a regular part of our firm's work process.

Now you may be wondering if we are just talking about good judgment here. Good judgment is certainly an element and should be used at all times, not just when making ethics evaluations. But good judgment is usually easier to identify after it has been put into practice, rather than the content of a cognizable strategy. Who would tell you good judgment is not part of their strategy? But it is so superfluous that it is rendered useless for shaping behavior. In order to make good judgment a strategy, we took a proactive approach to formalized ethics evaluations at points many lawyers fail to. We consider it consistently and ahead of time.

Another way of looking at our ethics strategy is to say that we don't wait until the last minute to start our assignment. We have a good friend who likes to say, "If you wait until the last minute to do something, it only takes you a minute to do it." While this may be suitable for cleaning your apartment, this procrastinator's strategy has seriously negative implications for many applications. If your college professor gives you an assignment with a due date well in the future and you get home for the afternoon and sit down and start to formulate your composition that same day, you are almost sure to periodically think about that assignment many times before you must hand in your assignment. Your brain isn't always thinking about the assignment, but it's always in the back of your head: the content of what you are writing, what you have written or what you want to change, and how you can get closer to making it the best piece of writing you've ever done. However, if you wait until the last minute, you won't have months of quality thought put into the assignment. In the months and weeks leading up to the due date, your brain will only be thinking, "Gee … I really need to start that assignment." There's not much benefit to your product from procrastination and worry.

We say our approach to ethics is similar to this "assignment" situation because when we proactively conduct ethics analysis from the beginning and consistently, our thoughts are consistently drawn back to the ethics of the matter. Our brains will keep the ethical considerations in the backs of our minds, rather than just be worrying, "Gee … we should look at the ethical rules about this sometime before we hand in our opinion." When we're proactive, we avoid missing the big ethical red flags.

You won't know every future eventuality, but focusing on ethics can inform your forecasting and force you to consider a possible outcome you might have initially ignored or discounted. Similarly, a very unlikely potential event could end up receiving greater weight (and less future discounting) when you consider its ethical implications up front, if those ethical implications have one or more very bad potential outcomes for your firm. For example, imagine that you are evaluating whether to engage as a silent member of a business venture with a client. Let's assume that you've become very close to this client, you trust them implicitly, and that the risk of the relationship turning sour appears to be extremely low. Yet while the likelihood of things going bad is minimal, if it were to occur, it could have potentially devastating effects on your law firm. From an ethical perspective, you may decide not to enter into that arrangement.

## HOW TO MAKE THE BEST ETHICAL CHOICES

Troublesome ethical concerns can arise in your practice in any number of ways, requiring your attention and time to sort through. But, for the sake of this discussion, let's get the obvious ones out of the way. (And our experience tells us that they're well worth mentioning.) As an ethics-conscious attorney, here's what you should and shouldn't do as a matter of course:

- Don't overbill your clients.
- Don't steal money from clients.
- Don't take on a matter that you can't figure out how to handle.
- Don't take on a matter and then neglect the work.
- Don't lie and don't help your clients lie.
- Don't break the law.
- Don't have sex with your clients. (In other words, don't be an idiot.)
- Do maintain your clients' files and data safely.
- Do meet every deadline.
- Do keep your clients' information confidential.

Beyond these ethical foundational cases, there are a range of other issues that land more in the gray area. They deal with unknowns, they aren't so obvious to identify in advance, and so they take more time and effort to sort through. Sometimes any path you choose can lead to poor outcomes, so you can only try to choose the least bad outcome. And as a practicing lawyer, you will inevitably be confronted with a variety of ethical choices to make.

For our practice, the more problematic ethical issues seem to fall into one of three categories, and they tend to present themselves over and over again. The first has to do with dealing with conflicts of interest that arise in the course of your work with multiple clients. The second occurs when you're deciding what to do about potentially questionable lawsuits. And the third category of tricky ethical issues arises when clients approach you wanting to find a "legal way" to do something that may or may not be legal. It's when they want you to try and find a way that they can get away with doing something with minimal risk – even though you both know that what they are doing is probably illegal.

## CONFLICTS OF INTEREST

As a business niche specialist lawyer, potential conflicts of interest will arise frequently simply due to the close nature of your business niche ecosystem. We take the attitude that potential conflicts of interest are a problem for us and our law firm because, if we don't avoid them, at some point we will be forced to pick sides, putting us in a "lose–lose" situation. It should go without saying, but as a small law firm, we never want to be in any "lose–lose" situation. So we try to look ahead and take action to avoid ever being in this type of position. To be proactive, whenever we take on new clients or new matters, we look at all the players involved and our relationship to them, and then try to foresee all of the potential conflicts of interest so we can avoid them.

Here's an example. One of our laboratory clients called us up to let us know that they had decided they wanted to sue their competitor, another laboratory. Now, we had never represented the competitor in question, but we were on retainer with one of that laboratory's service providers (arguably their most important service provider) – their medical billing company. We realized that we needed to think through whether it was appropriate and in everyone's best interest for us to even accept the matter. Because we had a relationship with that third party, we had to ask ourselves what might be the implications and possible ramifications of that relationship that could potentially be harmful to our client, the case, or to ourselves as a firm. For example, that third party could wind up being a witness to the lawsuit. They may be required to turn over documents to the court. Some of their billing practices might end up being at the heart of the lawsuit our clients were asking us to pursue for them. We realized that, even if no obvious conflicts occur, just by virtue of being in an adversarial position with that third party (a client of ours), the situation might cause us to need to terminate our relationship with them. What did we do? We took the case and we sued.

Another common example of potential conflicts of interest occurs when two independent businesses want to come together to form a joint venture and you have an existing relationship with both of them. Maybe the two businesses are getting along great and share a common vision, but down the road, it's still very possible that a conflict might arise. If that happens, you don't want to be in the position to say that you've decided to stick with one side over the other. If they end up suing each other, you can't represent either one of them against each other either because of your relationship with them.

If you do decide to move forward representing a joint venture, then go ahead and draft an arrangement, but be sure to obtain their informed consent in writing. Write to both parties and state that the purpose of the letter is to obtain their informed consent concerning your role in the joint venture activity that they're hiring you for. Then apprise them of the potential conflicts of interest. Explain that your law firm is not being hired to represent either of them, that you will be representing the joint venture. Also advise them to seek their own independent legal counsel to represent their individual rights. Make sure both parties understand that if their relationship does break down and either one decides to sue the other, that you can't represent either party against each other. By virtue of working with both sides, you'll have gained confidential information that could be used to the detriment of one client over the other.

And before you finalize anything, seek an independent, confidential review from your state bar, especially if it is your first time dealing with conflict of interest waivers. It's better to do it right the first time than learn on the fly, with potentially devastating consequences down the road.

Even if a client has given you express permission to do something on their behalf, you should still first evaluate whether it's worth it and whether it will be in the long-term interest of your firm to take on the matter. Sometimes clients are simply uncomfortable with you representing any competitor, even though there is no conflict of interest issue on the table or even on the horizon. Having an open conversation with clients about these feelings and making the decision not to represent a competitor in an unrelated matter can be used to build trust with that client. It could even help you in future negotiations regarding billing – although this shouldn't be a primary motivator. 'Look before you leap' is an understatement. If one of the parties approaching you has a track record of souring relationships that wind up in lawsuits, add that to your calculus and deeply consider the viability of the matter for your firm. If you know that this person often ends up in a lawsuit or on bad terms with their business partner, it might be smart to avoid that particular transaction at this time.

Clients are human beings. Sometimes human beings resort to unfairly blaming others for bad outcomes that happen to them. You never want a client to turn to you and tell you that because you did legal work for their competitor, they lost a contract or missed an opportunity that went to the competitor. Even if you did nothing wrong and complied with all ethical obligations, it could happen to you. You'd have to deal with the unpleasant outcome of them telling others within your industry that they don't think you are a loyal lawyer. Potential clients out there may not bother to hear your new business pitch if they have already heard these kinds of negative opinions from others, even if the accusations are leveled unfairly.

Again, it's not enough that your clients understand these principles, you simply must be sure that they are clearly communicated in writing. If any of this gets called into question and you find yourself in a position to have to defend yourself, then your defense will hinge on what you have recorded, signed, and documented.

If you do decide not to accept the joint venture assignment, let your clients know. They usually understand without much complaint. Let them know that ethical considerations prevent you from representing both of the parties in the matter. Doing so usually allows you to preserve the relationship with your client without them getting upset that you're declining to work on some of their matters.

When you're grappling with whether or not to take a case, or you find yourself in a position to have to pick a side, remember that you don't have to make your decision alone. Always check your state's rules and ethics opinions. When in doubt, get an official advisory from your state Bar Association. Be realistic: these are high-risk ventures and a lot of money is involved. You're going to have to sign your name to the pleadings, which could have significant consequences. It's not worth it to subject your law firm to a lot of risk to take on any one matter. On the other hand, it's easy to say no. Clients typically understand where you're coming from and even appreciate your transparency. Obviously, it sucks when your client has to hire a different lawyer or firm, but in the end, your declining a high-risk matter will avoid more problems than it creates. In the long run, they will continue to be a potential client if you treated them with respect and acted ethically.

## TO FILE OR NOT TO FILE

Clients file lawsuits for a variety of reasons, from settling rights of property and limiting the reach of their competitors to recovering large amounts of cash. For some clients, litigious efforts arise out of personal vendettas, emotion, even hatred. Others choose to file claims for less dramatic reasons like signaling their willingness to enforce agreements, proving that obligations included in contracts are legally enforceable, and setting an example for future situations, or perhaps even trying to get a discount on money they owe. Maybe a rogue employee has left and taken a client and the company wants to send a strong message that they'll have to deal with serious consequences if they don't abide by their employment agreement. An even murkier situation arises when they want to file a lawsuit that they don't fully intend to litigate through trial but wish to extract a higher settlement amount, even if they don't necessarily have a strong claim.

There will be many occasions when you will need to make an ethical judgment call about whether or not to file a suit for a client. But how do you decide which one is a go and which one is a no-go scenario? What ethical compass can you use to decide to file or not to file? Here's the formal Model Rule regarding making claims.

In the representation of a client, a lawyer shall not:

- file a suit, assert a position, conduct a defense, delay a trial, or take other action on behalf of the client when the lawyer knows or when it is obvious that such action would serve merely to harass or maliciously injure another;
- knowingly advance a claim or defense that is unwarranted under existing law, except that the lawyer may advance such claim or defense if it can be supported by good faith argument for an extension, modification or reversal of existing law.

This is your first guideline as a lawyer. The notes to the Model Rule go on to say, "The advocate has a duty to use legal procedure for the fullest benefit of the client's cause, but also a duty not to abuse legal procedure."

We've had a few situations like that. One business client had worked briefly with other lawyers before they came to us wanting to file a lawsuit against their former partners in a limited partnership. They wanted to move for an immediate interlocutory injunction, which would restrict the defendants' behavior during the trial until the case had been decided on the merits. They had a very, very strong claim against the other party for bad faith activity that had occurred about a year before they came to us. They claimed that their former partners had stolen insider information and numerous clients from them. The former partners seemed determined to continue causing immediate and irreparable harm to our client. Unfortunately, our client had waited a number of months before seeking attorneys to pursue legal action and by the time they came to us, a year had passed. On the face of it, they no longer seemed to have the legal grounds for receiving the interlocutory injunction. It was open to interpretation. Precedent was not altogether clear. There was an argument that the harm was ongoing, immediate and irreparable. The claim wasn't barred. It might have been stalled, but it was not "stale."

But our clients had a strong desire to move forward with the injunction, in addition to the underlying claims of the lawsuit. They told us they were willing to take any means necessary to prevent any further losses from their former partners. We could see that they had a legitimate claim for damages and were well within their rights to file a lawsuit. But, with the passage of time, they had lost their strong position in the matter of the injunction. Still, we felt we could argue their case about why irreparable harm still existed and needed to be addressed with an injunction. We just had to decide if it was the right thing to do.

You could make arguments for both sides: move for the injunction vs. don't move for it. On the one hand, you could argue that since a year had passed, there was no substantive reason to bring the motion anymore. But you could also argue that the bad actors were still engaged in the same behavior and still going after the accounts and other sensitive information about our client, and they needed to be stopped.

There was also another ethical point to consider. There's a difference between having an ethical obligation not to bring a claim because it is too risky for the client and not wanting to bring a claim because you don't think you can win it. That seemed to be the position of the client's previous lawyers. They didn't think they could win the injunction, so they caused further delays, until the client got fed up with them, undeterred, and came to us. But the other point that must be considered is that some attorneys work hard to maintain their reputations with judges. On the one hand, clients very much like selecting lawyers who know their way around the courts – sometimes even looking for attorneys who have a good reputation with the judge who's going to hear their case. On the other hand, no client wants to be the one whose case is declined by the law firm because that firm fears that taking the case would harm their reputation with the court.

Turns out, this is a very exploitable dynamic, which is especially useful for a smaller law firm starting out and having to compete with larger, more well-established law firms. Think of the "old boys' network." Some big firms stake themselves on their good relationships with judges. These good relations did not come by winning and/or fighting to the death for each and every one of their clients. The longevity of the relationship implies playing "nice," – compromising when necessary. And who lost in these compromises? Always some client, of course. Unless they expect to be in court many times for many different matters for a long time to come, that client doesn't need a good relationship with the judge. At best, you can neutralize the larger firm's advantage when they're competing with you for a client based on their perceived "local knowledge" and their good graces with the judge. You're not beholden to any "good old boy" understanding. You can fight to the death without pulling any punches to preserve a cozy relationship. And of course, clients like lawyers who fight for them.

It was a judgment call for us and we decided to take the risk and move for the injunction. The outcome was that we lost the injunction, but the lawsuit is still going on, and we are confident that we will win it.

There were a few downsides for us. We did lose the injunction. In the future, potential clients of ours might see the loss and it might be difficult for us to explain to them why the outcome was not as bad as it looks. It was a choice we made.

But even with the hit, we felt we made a net gain. At the end of the day, the client respected our tenacity and our action. They felt they finally had a law firm that was willing to fight for them. They felt the two firms they had tried before us hadn't done anything for them. In the long run, we still have the relationship with the client and they know that when they need a firm to get something done, we do it for them. We acted in our client's best interest.

Your next guideline as a lawyer is that you always want to be acting in the best interest of your clients. If a proposed lawsuit doesn't look like it has much merit and has necessarily little likelihood of winning, you have the ethical obligation to let your client know that. Decline to file it. As a lawyer, you're in the position of being something of a gatekeeper: you help your clients move forward on the lawsuits that have a fairly good likelihood of winning and you'll warn them if you believe their case doesn't warrant that.

But sometimes things aren't so black and white. Sometimes the client's best interests are served by proceeding with the case, in spite of the risk of loss. In other words, they may want to bring a lawsuit that they know has little merit, only because it makes business sense for them. In these situations, it might actually be in the best interest of your client to file the suit – contrary to your instincts. But you must have a good faith basis for believing you can win. There must be some set of circumstances, even if very unlikely, where your client wins the lawsuit. Your client may feel they need to override those concerns in order to accomplish something more pressing and more valuable. For example, sometimes companies are willing to spend the time, money, risk, and effort just to send a message to their organization, to their employees, or to the market, for that matter.

Especially when your client feels that their entire business is under threat, they might want to take legal action to right the wrong. They have an even bigger incentive to move forward with the action than to reduce their risk and not file, as you would normally advise.

You may even come across a client who wants to bring a suit that, from your perspective, is obviously without merit. Yet you must deliver that message to your client, along with your decision not to bring the claim, with careful tact. We've found the best way to handle this type of communication is to focus on objective factors related to the standard of evidence related to the type of claim. Review with your client the type of claims he intends to bring, or at least, the ones that most closely match his grievance and contemplated redress. Then list the evidence required to bring and/or win such claims. Objectively write down which elements or evidence they lack and put it to the client. Point out that he doesn't currently have enough evidence to meet the burden to bring such claims. You could even state that you are not opposed to bringing such a suit, but only if your client can produce the evidence necessary for you to move forward. If the client wants to continue arguing that he should still bring the case, you have an objective basis for declining representation, which hopefully should limit any hard feelings your client may have.

Framing your interaction this way points to the inadequacy of the *evidence*, not the inadequacy of your client or his intellect. You may even persuade your client to install mechanisms to preserve evidence of certain transactions ex ante in case he may need it later to convince you to bring a claim on his behalf. The point is that you have to decide what's right for you and how far you're willing to carry out the actions of your client. Plenty of lawyers will try to convince you that you need to tell your client what to do and what not to do. But that's not the issue here. You have to decide for yourself what constitutes acting in your client's best interest and proceed accordingly.

Communication is key. Be sure to take the time to talk to your client about what you're seeing in the case. Think through the ethical implications and possible outcomes with them. Don't assume that they have thought through the pros and cons, and potential wins and losses, for themselves. There will always be clients out there whose immediate reaction will be to litigate. It's your job to be the realist, the voice of reason, and the guide for best ethical behavior.

## HOW CAN I DO THIS [ILLEGAL] THING IN A LEGAL WAY?

Sometimes clients will approach you wanting to find out how they can get away with doing something that is very clearly not legal. When that happens, your ethical sensibilities need to kick in and you simply must decline the matter. While it might be an uncomfortable conversation to have, it's necessary; you don't have a choice if you want a future in law.

If the client is involved in any illegal activity, and you assist them in any way, or even if you simply know about it, it can be very damaging to you. You are opening yourself up to scrutiny of your legal work and all the ways in which the legal work you did affected or informed their illegal behavior. From a more selfish perspective, think of it this way: you never want to be the lawyer who represented the guy who eventually got investigated, arrested, or shut down for illegal activity. Public relations won't look good for the law firm, especially when you're in a small business niche. Just because it doesn't show up in the Wall Street Journal doesn't mean that your colleagues, your existing clients, and your potential clients aren't going to hear about it. They're going to hear about it.

But most of the time, you'll hear from clients who will tell you that they want to initiate a new venture or business activity and they want your help making sure that what they do is legal. Legal gray areas are fairly common – even more so in emerging business niches. If you're in a business niche that has extensive regulation, like we are, then not every regulation will cover every scenario. What is lawful is not always clearly delineated. And since you've now set yourself up as a problem-solver within your niche, you'll inevitably have business coming to you wanting your help making sure they're on the right side of the line.

We experience this regularly. New clients come to us and disclose that what they're doing seems to fall in a gray area, and they're not sure if it's allowable or not. They want our help finding a way to do what they do legally. So you have to make a judgment call based on the existing interpretations of these rules. What's legal and what's not?

When we talk to these kinds of clients, after doing our homework on the matter, we put our conclusions in a memo to our client. If we've determined that the answers fall in a gray area, then we let them know that the issue is open to interpretation and therefore has risk attached to it. We're clear that it appears that their actions may indeed run afoul of the law. And we put it in writing so there's no question that you have dutifully informed them.

## LEGAL OPINIONS

There will be times when it will be appropriate for you to formalize your conclusions with written opinions. If it's time to write an opinion, be sure to thoroughly consider all of the ethical and legal ramifications of the activity before you write the opinion. Hew to the ethical guidelines. Be sure that what you write, you can defend later. You might be writing an opinion today and two years from now you might find yourself defending it. If you don't think you would be able to get up in front of a judge and defend that opinion, then you shouldn't write it.

Let's say you were to analyze and research a business activity of a certain company, review all of the laws that potentially apply to it, and then write an opinion stating that the activity does not violate the law. If, after a year, the authorities bring a lawsuit against the company claiming that it did violate regulations after all, then your opinion will immediately come under scrutiny. At trial, your client can use your opinion letter as a part of his defense. Later, he may come after you, pointing out all the fines he's having to pay because he relied on your legal advice. Worse, the authorities could decide to bring a malpractice suit against you, and the government could try you for being complicit in the activity.

We found that the best way to avoid these kinds of outcomes is to clearly state that there is a chance that our client could be violating the law, regulation, or statute. We make it crystal clear that our opinions are issued only for that client and only that client can rely on our opinion. We don't know what anybody else is doing and we haven't investigated laws and regulations that apply to anyone else. So we are sure to clearly state who and what the opinion pertains to.

If your conclusion ends up being that the lawfulness of the activity really comes down to a subjective judgment call – then say that, too. "It's an open question. There isn't a direct precedent case on point that would make it clear one way or the other. It's open to interpretation." State the reasons you couldn't come to a definitive conclusion. And be sure to include verbiage stating that you can't guarantee the outcome, but this is what you would argue.

When you're in doubt about your conclusions, feel free to consult with the authorities. Most state bars have hotlines to answer questions and give informal opinions. If you do so and are later questioned about your final conclusions, you can say that you were aware of the potential ethics issues in the case, you consulted with the bar association, got an advisory opinion, and you decided what to do based on their input.

And then there are the clients themselves to be wary of. We've had our fair share of clients who came to us asking us to write opinion letters that would sanction an activity that fell in a gray area – or worse. Some want to engage you to have an excuse, and to be able to point their finger at a law firm and defend their actions retroactively. After some interactions, these folks become fairly easy to spot. They put you on calls with any number of potential partners or vendors and the sole reason you are on is to explain that you wrote an opinion stating that the behavior in question is "legal." They may have fired other previous counsel who wouldn't state the opinion they were seeking. And you might find that they've gotten one or more negative opinions from the other parties' counsel, with which this client obviously disagrees vehemently. When clients come to us with the sole intent of getting us to write an opinion letter – without any real interest in establishing a long-term relationship with us as a law firm – we're not interested. We decline work from those who essentially want an opinion letter to cover for whatever they are doing. It didn't take us long to recognize that these kinds of solicitations are big red flags.

There was one case in particular that we were grappling with. In the short term, it looked like a bad choice for our company to turn down what seemed to be a large amount of work. On the outside, it looked as if, by turning away the new client, we would hurt our business development and not benefit from some attractive fees. But in the long run, it served us to turn them down. That client ended up getting into numerous lawsuits with several businesses we had good relationships with. And they underwent investigations – which we completely expected. Now we can look back and proudly relate that we declined to represent that client thanks to our good judgment.

When you formulate your opinions, avoid potential problems by clearly stating the boundaries of your work. Explain your research and any absence of enforcement actions relating to the regulation or law. State any facts you assumed, along with any facts or matters you did *not* investigate, when you formulated your opinion. Be sure to restrict your opinion so that it only pertains to the date in question and only the specific matter that your opinion addresses. And if you refer to laws that are outside of the jurisdictions in which you are licensed, explain that you are not licensed there and that a lawyer that *is* licensed in that jurisdiction should be consulted. Finally, make it clear that only the client to whom the opinion is addressed may rely on this opinion.

In this chapter we've argued that taking a serious and proactive approach to ethics will help your business remain healthy for the long haul. We've discussed a few real-life examples of thorny ethics issues that are likely to be faced by your law firm and examined how to approach those issues and how taking the ethical approach serves the long-term interests of your firm. Consult your ethical compass frequently throughout the range of your law firm operations. Maintain the perspective that regular conversations about ethical concerns and long-term ramifications of ethical choices is not just good for your conscience – it's another tactic you'll need as a new small firm to steer you to the higher road of success.

In the next chapter, we will present ideas about how to sustain your new firm well into the future. Sustainability is often overlooked when all eyes are on handling cases and growing a new business, but if it is ignored, all the time, money, hopes, and work you've invested in your venture can be brought down fairly quickly. These will be the principles and practices of nurturing the long-term health of your new firm.

# 9. Building a sustainable practice

We were lucky we didn't lose everything that was important to us.

We were excited, driven, ambitious, and confident. It was our first year in business and we were working long, hard hours getting our firm up and running. We were doing everything we could to establish the infrastructure, build our client base, provide the legal services we were contracted for, and survive each month financially. But by the beginning of our second year, a pattern had developed that we weren't noticing. More than three months had passed without either one of us taking a full weekend off. We weren't sleeping enough, our diets consisted of snacks from the vending machine, daily heaping portions of greasy food from the food court a few buildings down the block, and enough alcohol each week to supply several prom parties. Our health started to show signs of deteriorating in front of our eyes. But it wasn't only our health we were ignoring; many things were slowly falling apart around us as well. Our personal relationships were taking a nosedive and we were starting to feel the heat from close friends and family around us. More, we were losing touch with others we cared for.

We finally looked at each other and realized that several patterns and behaviors we'd fallen into simply could not last. We were slowly destroying ourselves, so how could we effectively build and maintain a new business? While from several perspectives it seemed as if we were operating quite successfully, it dawned on us that some of our very critical "systems" in place were in danger of failing and could bring the entire enterprise down. And fast. It wasn't sustainable. No way could we maintain that pace for much longer.

We had placed our firm at great risk. We were stretched too thin, understaffed, and had no contingency plans. Anything could have happened. One of us could have gotten sick. We could have had a tough break in one of our lawsuits, our biggest case could have disappeared, or countless other things could have taken us down. But, thankfully, we woke up to our situation before anything fell apart. Soon enough, we hired an intern and began sharing some of the burden. As we began to right the ship, nothing irreparable happened: our health returned over time, our relationships with our loved ones survived, and our relationship with each other stayed on an even keel. But in hindsight, we realized that we took things to the edge of a cliff. We consider ourselves extremely lucky that nothing important to us was destroyed.

What happened? How – with all of our education, savvy, and early success – could we have gotten so close to the brink without even recognizing it? What huge piece of the puzzle – the lack of which almost brought us down in very short order – had we missed?

We have come to think of it as *sustainability*. And it's not surprising that we missed it. There continues to be an unfortunate lack of focus on sustainability in the existing law literature and practice management focus. Yet sustainability is a deceptively important component for any law firm that not only wants to succeed, but wants to stay healthy and successful for many years to come.

In this chapter, we will discuss perspectives on sustainability that are drawn from our own experiences, and the hard-won insights that sometimes come only from learning things the hard way. We'll point out why sustainability issues can be easy to overlook for anyone focused on getting a new law firm launched. We'll try to define what sustainability is, and how it can be recognized. And finally, we'll share strategies that we have used for nurturing sustainability and neutralizing factors that can threaten your law firm's health and longevity.

## ANYONE CAN MISS IT

We weren't the only company that underestimated the importance of keeping an eye out for sustainable practices. Uber, the ubiquitous ride-sharing technology company, was launched in 2010 by three friends in San Francisco and leapt to success within its first year of providing an alternative to taxicabs. The founders built a highly profitable business on great technology and generated a lot of revenue. But in the summer of 2017, one of their founders was ousted as CEO owing to a seeming variety of issues including poor and ethically suspect business practices. It wasn't until Uber's public image and perceived value had taken a huge hit that their organization began to wake up to how critical issues of sustainability are to a company's success.

To most outside observers, the issues that came to the fore in 2017 for Uber were the result of a series of individual bad decisions and poor "culture." We would argue that these in turn were the result of a lack of focus on sustainability. It is a very large and public example of what happens when a company fails to focus on sustainability until well after they've established themselves in the marketplace. In other words, those in charge took Uber to the edge. They played fast and loose with ethics and legalities. They have been accused of failing to be transparent about their use of secret tracking software and failing to cooperate with criminal investigations involving their drivers, and as a result, they lost their permission to operate in London. They allegedly paid off hackers who stole personal data from all of its 50 million+ users and then tried to cover up the hack. As of this writing, they are embroiled in litigation with the self-driving car technology group, Waymo, over alleged clandestine attempts to compete, involving theft of trade secrets.

What's the lesson here? Happy with their success and growth, Uber executives appear to have neglected to consider the long-term picture and failed to weigh their business choices on the scale of sustainability. They didn't recognize that sustainability could well be one of the most important and yet underappreciated business objectives for any business. And they are not alone. There are many stories of businesses that didn't think to secure their long-term story and paid dearly for the oversight.

We lawyers may be especially susceptible to overlooking the issue. When you're in the early stages of getting your new small law firm off the ground, it's not the first agenda item on your list. It's compelling to focus on your sexier, more growth-focused goals like capturing new clients, defining your brand, designing your organizational structure, hiring, and so on. The instinct for survival propels you forward and adrenaline kicks in as things get in gear and you think you might actually make a business out of your practice. Just getting the ball rolling feels like a huge success.

And most of us are over-achieving, hard working, driven professionals who have invested a lot of our personal resources – time, money, energy, passion – to get where we are. Yet while being obsessed with success can sometimes open doors for us, it can also make us blind to the fact that our boat is taking on water.

Our work is highly stressful; there's always one more thing to worry about. So the stress can build quickly, take a mental toll, and have unfortunate consequences. Just check the statistics. Lawyers are 3.6 times more likely to suffer from depression than other professions. Reportedly 18–20% of lawyers abuse drugs, compared with 8–10% of the general population. And there are plenty of examples of lawyers who've gone off the deep end both within big firms and in private practices largely owing to the stressful nature of the work.

So as lawyers, we might be even more likely than other professionals to miss the warning signs that our firms are being threatened from unseen factors from within. If we do miss it, we'll then be forced to confront it, at some point, usually not on our terms. The energy and excitement of those first few months or years won't last and won't be enough to build a thriving, well-run, long-lasting business. We inevitably will be compelled to switch our vision from a dreamy focus on surviving to a broader focus of being sustainable. We'll have to stop being consumed with the question, "How can we keep it from failing?" and begin to start asking, "How can we make this last?"

The truth is that sustainability *is essential to* survival; we can't have the latter without the former. If you can't effectively keep operating status quo, your entire firm can go away tomorrow.

## WHAT IS SUSTAINABILITY?

The term *sustainability* seems to be everywhere these days. It's a term that everyone seems to think they understand, but very few have a good grasp of what it means. It's nebulous and imprecise, a buzzword that gets peppered into almost every conversation.

While the word seems to imply a concern with longevity when it is applied to the health of a business, it's not clear if it pertains to growth or survival. Or both at the same time. Does it depend on the business? Is it a long- or short-term concern? Or is it all-term? Is it about healthy balance or healthy boundaries? Where do you find it? How do you cultivate it? And on and on.

The dictionary's not much help, either. Two definitions that immediately pop up (in a Google search, of course) include: "The ability to be sustained" and "Capable of being supported." These are clearly not much help. The most useful definition to apply to the business of law might come from authorities on biology, where they define sustainability as, "the property of systems to remain diverse and productive indefinitely." This definition seems to be the closest to our concept of having a sustainable law firm. By "diverse" here, we mean that a firm should diversify its legal skills and the types of matters it undertakes while focusing only on a specific business niche in order to leverage expertise to grow the firm.

Another complication in our quest for sustainability is that practices to cultivate sustainability will certainly vary within industries, among businesses, and from one firm to the next. We won't be able to give you a one-size-fits-all model that you can apply to your firm. There's no rigid, universally applicable formula. What works for one may actually threaten the sustainability of another. We want you to master a diversity of legal skills and a variety of types of legal matters as you maintain a laser-like focus on a particular business niche and its clients. Niches differ, as do people. Two different people applying these same lessons to a different business niche will generate very different stories.

We believe that sustainability needs to be an integral part of your business model for your firm to get taken seriously right from the beginning of your launch. Think about it. Why do clients continue to flock to those tired, old, stodgy law firms to get help with their legal concerns? It's very likely that what makes them so attractive is that they project one specific and highly valuable quality: sustainability. They've proven that they are not just winning their biggest cases – they are managing their business, their clients, and their cases well enough to survive decade after decade. Companies and clients value this level of sustainability because it reduces their risk. It justifies their general counsel's decision to hire an outside law firm, citing, "If big, profitable, and thriving companies pay a lot of money to retain this old law firm, then our company should be in a good position to thrive by hiring that firm as well." On the other hand, examples of companies who are thriving owing to working with a dynamic, cost-effective niche law firm are less visible on first blush.

As a brand new small law firm, you're going to be fighting an uphill battle against this dynamic, which is why learning to view your firm's operations and practices through the lens of sustainability is critical to your growth and business development. New clients will want to know that, if they hire you today, you'll be around for the years ahead to litigate, appeal, or settle their case – just as much as any of those old and rusty, big-name firms we discussed earlier. If prospective clients are in the early stages of building their own businesses, their cases could easily last for years – they'd rather go hire someone else if they have any fear that you won't be by their side in the years to come. Once you've earned an air of sustainability, you will be much more valuable in the eyes of your prospective clients.

## STRATEGIES TO BUILD SUSTAINABILITY

What systems, patterns, activities, or behaviors aren't functioning well within your firm? Or your life? Which of them might break down over time, and as a result, bring other things down with it? Look around you. Are there any warning signs of dysfunction? If the rest of your life is falling apart, then you don't have a sustainable practice. If your loved ones are complaining about never seeing you, then you don't have a sustainable practice. If your health is deteriorating and you don't have time to go to the doctor or take care of yourself, there's something about your practice that's not sustainable. It's time to wake up and smell the single-origin, craft-java house coffee.

You also can't predict when the reality of your firm's habit of ignoring issues of sustainability will rear its head and demand your attention. Unfortunately, the signs are easy to miss. And if you don't recognize unsustainable practices for what they are until they start to take you down, it may be too late. So instead of waiting for catastrophe, we recommend that you integrate practices into your firm right from the start that address a concern for sustainability. Become determined to root out what might hamper your long-term health. Watch for warning signs and ask the right questions.

Keeping an eye on sustainability means that you look for the habits, practices, and expectations that can bring down the business, if not corrected. Unfortunately, there aren't replicable practices that ensure sustainability from one firm to the next. We're not going to be able to point out specific business practices and say, "Why, yes. These are clearly the characteristics of a sustainable enterprise." But we are going to point you in the direction of what is *not* sustainable so that you can begin to recognize problems before they cause any damage and rectify them in your own way. In essence, we can help you remove the obstacles to your firm's long-term health.

Hopefully, you will integrate a focus on sustainability early on in your business development so you don't end up like us, or Uber, scrambling to put things in place belatedly to save your company from imploding. Do it right from the beginning and enjoy your law firm's successes for years to come. Here are a few strategies to get you started.

## Hold Regular Conversations about Sustainability

Once we figured out that we needed to think about sustainability – shocker! – we began to talk regularly and frequently about it for our firm. From that point on, it became the lens through which we viewed all material decisions for our practice. We recommend that you do the same. Start sprinkling your days and weeks with conversations about it. Allocate 10 minutes of your weekly meetings to consider what might be threatening your sustainability at that point in time. Think about how you can resolve the issue or avoid it in the future. Start with what's closest to home. How's your mental and physical health? Is it sustainable? How are your relationships? Are they suffering owing to overwork?

Or, you can go with a more formal approach and set up annual or bi-annual sustainability reviews. Like your annual physical, you can use it as a checkpoint to see if everything is working in good order and that no practices or behaviors are being overlooked that could risk the health of the firm for the long term.

## Manage your Time, Resources and Expectations

Sustainability is about managing uncertainty. You really don't know how much time anything is going to take; you don't know how much time a type of matter, or any specific matter, is going to take. Part of your growth process will be about assessing, learning, and adjusting your schedules and processes to accommodate floating deadlines and project "creep." To get in front of it, you'll need to observe and manage your time and resources, as well as your expectations.

Look around your organization right now. What is in place temporarily to fill a gap, but might wear down in short order? What is good for the short run but won't last in the long run?

## Get Perspective

A lot of lawyers love to get lost in the details and plow through what's in front of them. It's easy to assume that if everyone is busy then everything is good. Don't make the mistake of thinking that as long as you're not sitting around with nothing to do, then everything is fine.

In fact, it can be quite valuable to elicit perspectives from those who don't have an emotional or financial investment in the health of your firm. One of the reasons we woke up to our condition was that some of our friends started telling us that we looked haggard. That got us thinking. Consider bringing in an independent person every once in a while to help review your firm's sustainability health. It can be illuminating to get an outside perspective. When you're running your firm, you see everything up close and it's hard to see the bigger perspective. You can't really see the forest for the trees, as they say.

An objective observer can be worth their weight in gold. Invite someone to be the devil's advocate and poke holes in your theory of why your business is so excellent. You don't have to spend thousands of dollars to get some fresh insights. But ideally, you'll have someone with some business experience to take a look under the hood, kick the tires, and give you feedback about might be threats to your firm's sustainability as they see them.

## Do an Ethics Check

Simply put, the more risk you take with ethics, the less likely your firm will be sustainable. Participating in greedy or unethical actions and tactics is probably the fastest and surest way to threaten your new law firm's long-term survival. Greed and lack of ethics go hand in hand: if you're taking ethics risks, you're probably doing it because you want to make more money, and you're willing to bend the rules a little to do so. But in the end, greed and poor ethics are a losing proposition. Probably the majority of lawyers who've been disbarred were disbarred owing to greedy behavior. Taking ethical risks is like playing with fire. Eventually something will blow up in your face and probably bring everything down with you.

**Your Sustainability Toolkit**

To get you started with an honest review of your firm's sustainability, here's a set of questions to ask yourself, your partner, and anyone else in your firm. Again, this is just the beginning. Ask open-ended questions so that you can discover the threats that no one would think of:

- **Health**. How's my health? Am I getting enough rest? How are my relationships with my family and friends? If I take a vacation next week could the firm still run the way it should? Am I overtired? Overworked? How's my mental health?
- **Clients**. What if we lose our biggest client tomorrow? How would we deal with it? How can we be less dependent on that one client?
- **Cases**. What if our biggest case settled tomorrow? Could we still pay the bills? What can we do to bolster our financial safety? Would that client come back to us for another matter in the future? Will that client ever have legal needs again?
- **Ethics**. Are we acting greedily in any situation? If so, what sort of ethics risks are we incurring for the firm? Are there signs or evidence of greed anywhere that we haven't noticed yet?
- **What else?** Is there anything else about our firm that makes our productivity vulnerable over time such that it cannot be carried well into the future?

\* \* \*

After all that you have invested in building your new law firm, make sure that you build sustainability into your game plan so you can keep it around for a long time. Make sustainability a business objective as much as increasing profit margin, a high public profile, and having a high win ratio. And enjoy the fruits of your labor over the many years of success that lie ahead of you.

# Index